IMAGES
of America

WARSHIPS AT SEAWOLF PARK

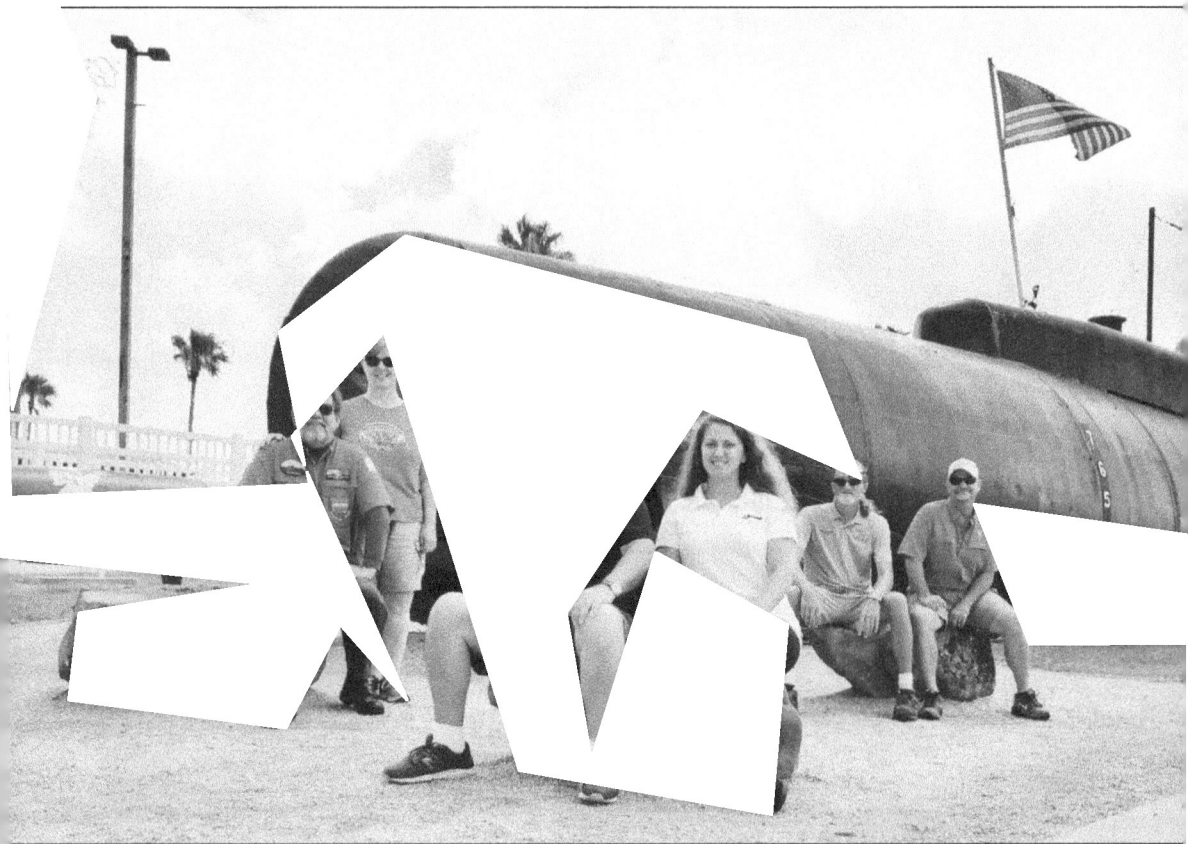

For over 45 years, the professional staff and volunteers of the American Undersea Warfare Center, Galveston's Naval Museum on Pelican Island have restored and preserved the historic warships of Seawolf Park. (Kelley Crooks.)

ON THE COVER: Historic World War II submarine USS *Cavalla* sits next to her sister ship USS *Stewart* at the American Undersea Warfare Center at Seawolf Park. Both are open for tours daily. (Kelley Crooks.)

IMAGES
of America

WARSHIPS AT
SEAWOLF PARK

Col. Kelley Crooks, USAF (Ret.)
and Mark Lardas

ARCADIA
PUBLISHING

Copyright © 2018 by Col. Kelley Crooks, USAF (Ret.) and Mark Lardas
ISBN 978-1-5402-3663-0

Published by Arcadia Publishing
Charleston, South Carolina

Library of Congress Control Number: 2018946705

For all general information, please contact Arcadia Publishing:
Telephone 843-853-2070
Fax 843-853-0044
E-mail sales@arcadiapublishing.com
For customer service and orders:
Toll-Free 1-888-313-2665

Visit us on the Internet at www.arcadiapublishing.com

*To our servicemen and women who sacrificed some, or all, in
the past for the freedoms we each enjoy today. Thank you.*

*In Memoriam
Capt. Ernest "Zeke" Zellmer, USN (Ret.)
(May 31, 1921–August 27, 2018)
"On Eternal Patrol"*

CONTENTS

ACKNOWLEDGMENTS

The authors are very proud of this book; many loving family and friends of those courageous sailors who braved the elements and the enemy to preserve our liberty during World War II contributed immensely to the personal impact of the story inside. Those who have helped so much include the staff of the Cavalla Historical Foundation, especially Aubrey Flaherty and Dr. K. Anderson Crooks for photography and access to many wonderful artifacts; the Edsall-class Veterans Association and the US Submarine Veterans Inc. for great before and after restoration photographs; and William Lardas for accompanying Mark on many of his trips and doing photography, as he has in Mark's last four Arcadia books.

We would also like to thank Caitrin Cunningham and Lindsey Givens, our editors at Arcadia Publishing, for their assistance.

Mark wishes to express his love and appreciation for his late wife, Janet Lardas, who passed while he was working on this book. They were married for over 40 years. During his writing career, Janet's unconditional support and encouragement kept him going. "I miss her deeply."

Kelley wishes to express his thanks to those who inspire him every day—his parents, Ken and Kathy Crooks; his daughters, Kiyra and Karly; and especially, Patricia Lapsley, who "makes me take in the sunlight every day."

The following abbreviations indicate the sources of the illustrations used in this volume:

AF	Photograph by Aubrey Flaherty
AUWC	American Undersea Warfare Center archives
BT	Photograph by Barbie Tootle
CE	Photograph by Chip Engler and Laurie Engler
DRKC	Photograph by Dr. Kerry Crooks, PhD
GO	Photograph by George Obern
KC	Author Kelley Crooks's collection of images
LOC	Library of Congress
ML	Author Mark Lardas's collection of images
NARA	National Archives and Records Administration
RB	Photograph by Richard Bruns
RM	Donated by Ruth Meier
RS	Photograph by Ruth Steitle
USNHHC	US Naval History and Heritage Command

INTRODUCTION

In October 1998, Galveston's city leaders considered abandoning the ship and submarine museum located at beautiful Seawolf Park on historic Pelican Island. "What would it take to get rid of those ships and convert that space to an RV park?" Today, the septuagenarian Gato-class USS *Cavalla* (SS-244) submarine and the Edsall-class destroyer escort (DE) USS *Stewart* (DE-238) remain, reminding passing ships and visitors of the sacrifices made by World War II sailors.

Their story was part of the Allies' successful plan to win in the Pacific against the Imperial Japanese Navy and in the frigid North Atlantic against German U-Boat "wolf packs."

On its initial patrol in 1944, a young crew aboard *Cavalla* left Pearl Harbor, headed toward history and Tokyo Bay in 1945. There, they witnessed the signing of the Japanese Instrument of Surrender aboard the battleship USS *Missouri*. At the same time, USS *Stewart* protected allied convoys from the Arctic to the Caribbean Seas. *Stewart* also served as a training ship and escorted Pres. Franklin Delano Roosevelt's yacht traveling to meet with Winston Churchill, Joseph Stalin, and Chiang Kai-shek in the Middle East.

Their stories begin in the 1940s. The story of Seawolf Park and Pelican Island begins a century earlier as a salt marsh in the early 1800s. North of Galveston, Pelican Island grew collecting silt and soil, eventually combining with another salt marsh, Pelican Spit, to become a 7.5-square-mile barrier island.

In the 1830s, Galveston became Texas's major immigration center, the "Ellis Island of the West." People fleeing poverty and persecution brought the threat of disease like yellow fever, so Texas established Pelican Island as a quarantine station. Many Jewish immigrants, sponsored by the Jewish Immigrants Information Bureau, were redirected to Galveston because New York authorities felt too many Jews were coming through Ellis Island.

After the Civil War, yellow fever again hit Galveston and for the next 50 years, quarantine stations were built, destroyed by hurricanes, and rebuilt. Finally, in 1915, a federal facility was built and lasted until it closed in 1950 after processing millions of immigrants into the United States.

By the time our warships at Seawolf Park were commissioned, the United States was deep into World War II and the US War Department was energizing the American industrial base. Over 560 destroyer escorts, divided into six classes (depending on differences in size, armament, and propulsion), were designed and built between 1943 and 1945. USS *Stewart* was the first Edsall-class destroyer escort built by the Brown Shipbuilding Company in Houston. Launched on November 22, 1942, and after six months of training, *Stewart* was commissioned on May 31, 1943, under the command of Lt. Comdr. B.C. Turner, US Navy Reserve.

Stewart was the third naval vessel named after Adm. Charles Stewart (1778–1869). A US Navy officer, Admiral Stewart commanded the historic frigate *Constitution*, "Old Ironsides." The other two *Stewarts* were the Bainbridge-class destroyer USS *Stewart* (DD-13) and Clemson-class destroyer USS *Stewart* (DD-224). DD-13 served from its commissioning in 1902 through World War I, where she saw action against German U-boats. DD-224, commissioned September 15, 1920, supported US Marines in the Second Sino-Japanese War, and later in World War II, when she was severely damaged during the Battle of Badung Strait in February 1942. She put into Surabaya for repairs but was scuttled when the port came under enemy attack. The Japanese raised DD-224 and commissioned her as patrol boat No. 102. Patrol boat No. 102 escorted convoys in Japan's Southwest Area Fleet and reportedly was involved in the sinking of the USS *Harder* (SS-257).

USS *Stewart* (DE-238) took her initial cruise in June 1943 to New Orleans. There, she joined the Atlantic Fleet under the Operational Training Command. For the next four months, *Stewart* trained and certified student Navy officers from Miami to Cuba to Norfolk. In October 1943, USS *Stewart*, with senior military staff aboard, escorted the presidential yacht down the Potomac River to Chesapeake Bay where passengers transferred to the battleship USS *Iowa*, which took them all to the historic Tehran Conference.

Over the next 19 months, USS *Stewart* continued as a trainer and escorted over 30 convoys transiting the Atlantic. Most missions went without incident, tracking German U-boats and enduring the bitter North Atlantic seas. However, on April 10, 1945, *Stewart* found herself off the coast of New York when she was called to assist the tanker SS *St. Mihiel*. With over eight million gallons of aviation fuel on board, *St. Mihiel* was rammed amidships by the SS *Nashbulk*. Flames swept the deck, leaving no time to man life boats. The crew "headed to the rails," but 27 crewmen never made it over the side. *Stewart* fought the blaze, dispatched crew and firefighters on board the *St. Mihiel*, reestablished power, and fired up the engines. Surviving merchant crewmen were rescued from the frigid waters, sufficient operations were established, and the *Stewart* escorted *Nashbulk* back to New York while the USS *Edsall* (DE-129) escorted the St. Mihiel.

In June 1945, USS *Stewart* went through the Panama Canal en route to San Diego and was ordered to Pearl Harbor. With sister ships *Edsall*, *Moore* (DE-240), and *Wilhoite* (DE-397), *Stewart* arrived at Pearl Harbor on August 4, where they trained with the USS *Spearfish* (SS-190) and cruiser USS *Baltimore* (CA-68). Scuttlebutt was that *Stewart* was training for picket duty off the coast of Japan to fight off kamikazes during the Allied invasion of Japan's mainland. Hiroshima, Nagasaki, and Japan's surrender rendered the training moot. After the war, *Stewart* returned to San Diego, then back to the East Coast. Placed into the Atlantic Reserve Fleet in Philadelphia and then decommissioned in January 1947 at Green Cove Springs, Florida, *Stewart* changed berthing areas three times over the next two decades, ending up back home in Orange, Texas. In 1972, she was inspected and deemed unfit for naval service. *Stewart* was stricken from the Navy Register, and two years later, she was donated to the City of Galveston as a museum display to be located on Pelican Island, to sit beside another World War II warrior, USS *Cavalla*.

The other warship at Seawolf Park is the Gato-class submarine USS *Cavalla*. Named for a torpedo-shaped mackerel fish, *Cavalla* was built by the Electric Boat Company in Groton, Connecticut, and launched on November 14, 1943. Sponsored by the wife of Rear Adm. Merrill Comstock, her commissioning was moved to February 29, 1944. Her superstitious crew felt that date, a leap day, would bring them good luck. Since she continues to serve America to this day at Seawolf Park, she's truly a "Lucky Lady."

Cavalla conducted six Pacific war patrols commanded by Lt. Comdr. Herman Kossler. Between her April 11, 1944, departure from New London until she witnessed the Japanese surrender in Tokyo Bay on September 2, 1945, *Cavalla* logged almost 90,000 nautical miles and sank 34,180 tons of enemy shipping.

Cavalla's first patrol spanned 64 days from May 31 to August 3, 1944. Leaving Pearl Harbor, *Cavalla* sailed to her duty station east of Luzon, the largest Philippine island. Ordered to rendezvous with USS *Pipefish* (SS-388), they deployed in search of a Japanese task force that was heading toward Saipan in the Mariana Islands some 2,600 kilometers away. *Cavalla* went looking for a very large needle in an even larger haystack.

On June 14, their first night out, *Cavalla* made radar contact: a small convoy of two large tankers and three destroyers. Without engaging, they were discovered and forced to dive and escape; this was not the task force in question. The very next day, *Cavalla* was heading southwest when they again made radar contact. This time, they identified multiple carriers, three battleships, a dozen cruisers, and two dozen destroyers in the Japanese fleet heading to Saipan. Lieutenant Commander

Kossler ordered *Cavalla* to dive, allowing the task force to pass overhead. She resurfaced and followed the task force for two days, radioing their position until, on June 17, Kossler transmitted their position before diving to avoid detection by enemy aircraft overhead.

That fleet was intercepted on June 19–20, and the Battle of the Philippine Sea, also known as the "Marianas Turkey Shoot," commenced. For her part, *Cavalla* spotted the Japanese aircraft carrier *Shokaku* as she recovered aircraft. Kossler fired a full spread of six torpedoes yielding three direct hits. *Cavalla* was the only submarine to avenge Pearl Harbor, and her crew was awarded the Presidential Citation for her actions.

On July 1, *Cavalla* returned to Saipan and stayed about two miles out between the islands of Saipan and Tinian. The crew witnessed Japanese and Allied forces battling ashore. In his diary, *Cavalla* crew member William Bates wrote, "We stood on the bridge with glasses and could see the whole battle. We watched the landing forces, planes making bomb runs, and cruisers shelling shore positions. [We] could see Jap tanks, trucks, and men. Saw two plane[s] shot down and 2 Jap shore batteries blown sky high. In the afternoon, we went over the side for a swim for about two hours. It really felt good. Everybody else thought we were crazy!"

Dangers lurked all around on patrol. If she was not diving in under 30 seconds to avoid aircraft strafing or bombing, or enemy destroyers dropping depth charges, *Cavalla* also dealt with floating mines. On February 24, two weeks into their fourth patrol, *Cavalla* sighted an object passing down its port side. It was "a nice little mine," which was followed by other mines. *Cavalla* found herself in a mine field. Mines were typicaliy spaced in rows 400–500 feet apart, situated far enough apart to avoid a mass detonation. Kossler zig-zagged through the field "like a snake in a corn field" the rest of the night, allowing the crew to detonate them by firing on them.

So it went for 19 months. *Cavalla* and her crew would detect, identify, and attack, all while avoiding detection, identification, and attack—cat and mouse, predator and prey. Even after a cease fire was given on August 15, 1945, *Cavalla* had to evade a lone Japanese plane dropping bombs on them. She dove out of danger and later notified Pacific Fleet that some Japanese forces might not know the war was over. After the war, *Cavalla* returned to New London and was placed into the Reserve Fleet on March 16, 1946.

The US Navy donated USS *Cavalla* and USS *Stewart* to Seawolf Park in the early 1970s. Insufficient maintenance, public vandalism, and multiple hurricanes severely deteriorated both ships. The US Navy and the City of Galveston almost gave up on them. A few staunch old salts, the Submarine Veterans of Texas, and the Cavalla Historical Foundation conducted significant restoration so that *Stewart* was listed in the National Register of Historic Places on July 12, 2007, followed by *Cavalla* on May 27, 2008.

The staff and volunteers at Seawolf Park continue the restoration battle, preserving history, memorializing those who fought, and educating the public on the life of our World War II sailors and submariners. With continued support from the City of Galveston, the warships at Seawolf Park will celebrate their centennial at Pelican Island.

Pictured under the bright light of the planet Venus is the American Undersea Warfare Center naval museum portion of Seawolf Park. USS *Stewart*, with her wheelhouse lights lit, sits on the far side (starboard side) of USS *Cavalla*. (KC.)

One

HISTORY OF SEAWOLF PARK

Seawolf Park is located on the eastern tip of Pelican Island, just North of Galveston Island, Texas. Pelican Island sits between Galveston Bay and the Gulf of Mexico. Visitors routinely see shipping, ferry boats, and fishing trawlers traversing the Galveston Channel. Off the northeast end of the park lies the SS *Selma*, a 425-foot-long World War I–era tanker made of concrete—the largest of its kind.

With sub-tropical marshes, estuaries, fresh and saltwater inlets, and harbors all sitting between Galveston Bay and the Gulf of Mexico, Seawolf Park is known for its great fishing. Fish of many varieties (drum, catfish, flounder, and redfish) make their way past Pelican Island. Videos have documented fish as long as three feet being caught.

This is a unique place where visitors can come to fish, play, and barbecue at playgrounds and picnic areas, and visit a World War II naval museum. The museum is a memorial to its namesake, the submarine USS *Seawolf*, as well as the other 51 submarines, 374 officers, and 3,100 crewmen lost at sea during World War II. The museum houses the USS *Cavalla* submarine and USS *Stewart* destroyer escort, the sail of the USS *Tautog*, and the conning tower of the submarine USS *Carp*.

On September 18, 1978, the first "crossing of bows" occurred as the nuclear submarine USS *Cavalla* (SSN-68) entered the Port of Galveston in front of the World War II submarine USS *Cavalla* (SS-244). As they passed, the SSN-68 Navy crew saluted the SS-244 Texas Navy Junior ROTC crew.

Hurricanes like Ike (2008) and Harvey (2017) forced changes on the island and at the naval museum. In 1974, the museum included an FJ-4 Navy Fury fighter, an Army tank, and a Marine Corps Armored Personnel Carrier (APC). Each of these artifacts has long since been removed or washed away. In all her configurations, Seawolf Park and the naval museum continue to bring history to Galveston Island.

During the infancy of Seawolf Park, around 1971, crews had USS *Cavalla* floated into her cradles prior to many other park structures. Three years later, USS *Stewart* was added, pushed into place on Cavalla's starboard side by the tug *Linda Fisher*. (AUWC.)

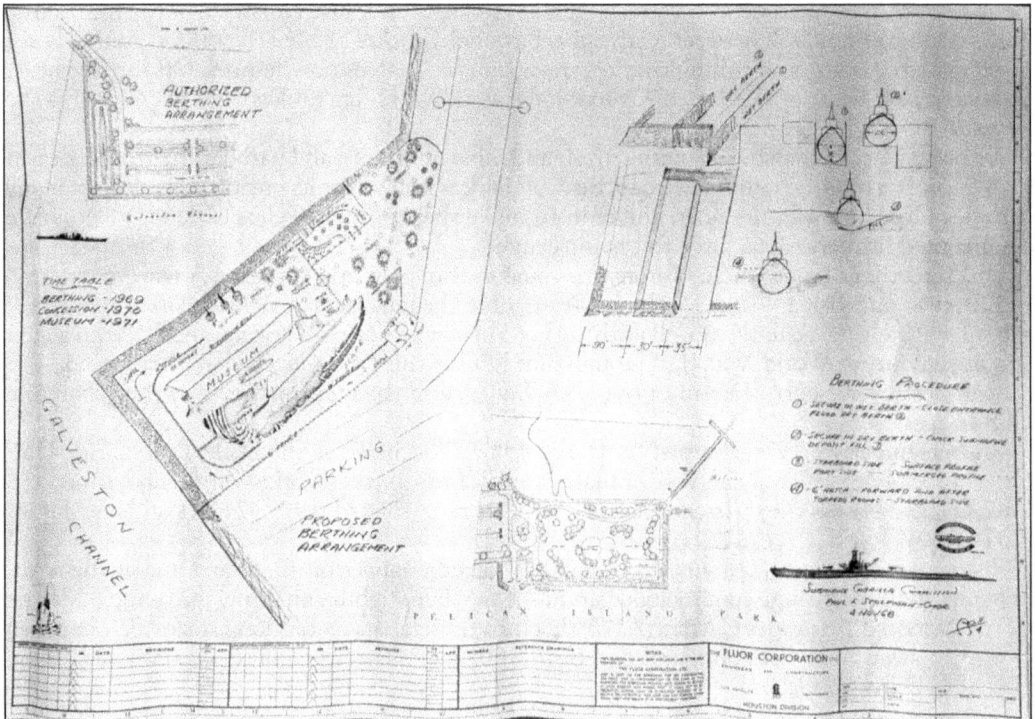

Early engineering plans of Pelican Island Park by the Fluor Corporation in 1968 showed the Balao-class submarine USS *Cabrilla*, not USS *Cavalla*, berthed next to a museum building and picnic area. These plans depict the procedures for positioning the submarine into her dry berth. (AUWC.)

Galveston, Texas

This late 1970s Seawolf Park postcard shows that the naval museum at the time included an FJ-4 Fury jet aircraft and bamboo huts (near the stern of USS *Stewart*), and the park included the Seawolf Park pavilion and bait shops. The jet was damaged under the surge of Hurricane Ike in 2008. (AUWC.)

The aircraft at Seawolf Park, commonly believed to be an F-86 Sabre, was in fact an FJ-4 Fury, built by North American Aviation in the 1950s to 1960s. The Sabre was a Korean War–era Air Force fighter, while the Fury was a Navy swept-wing, carrier-capable fighter-bomber. A total of 1,115 Furies were produced for the Navy and Marine Corps. (AUWC.)

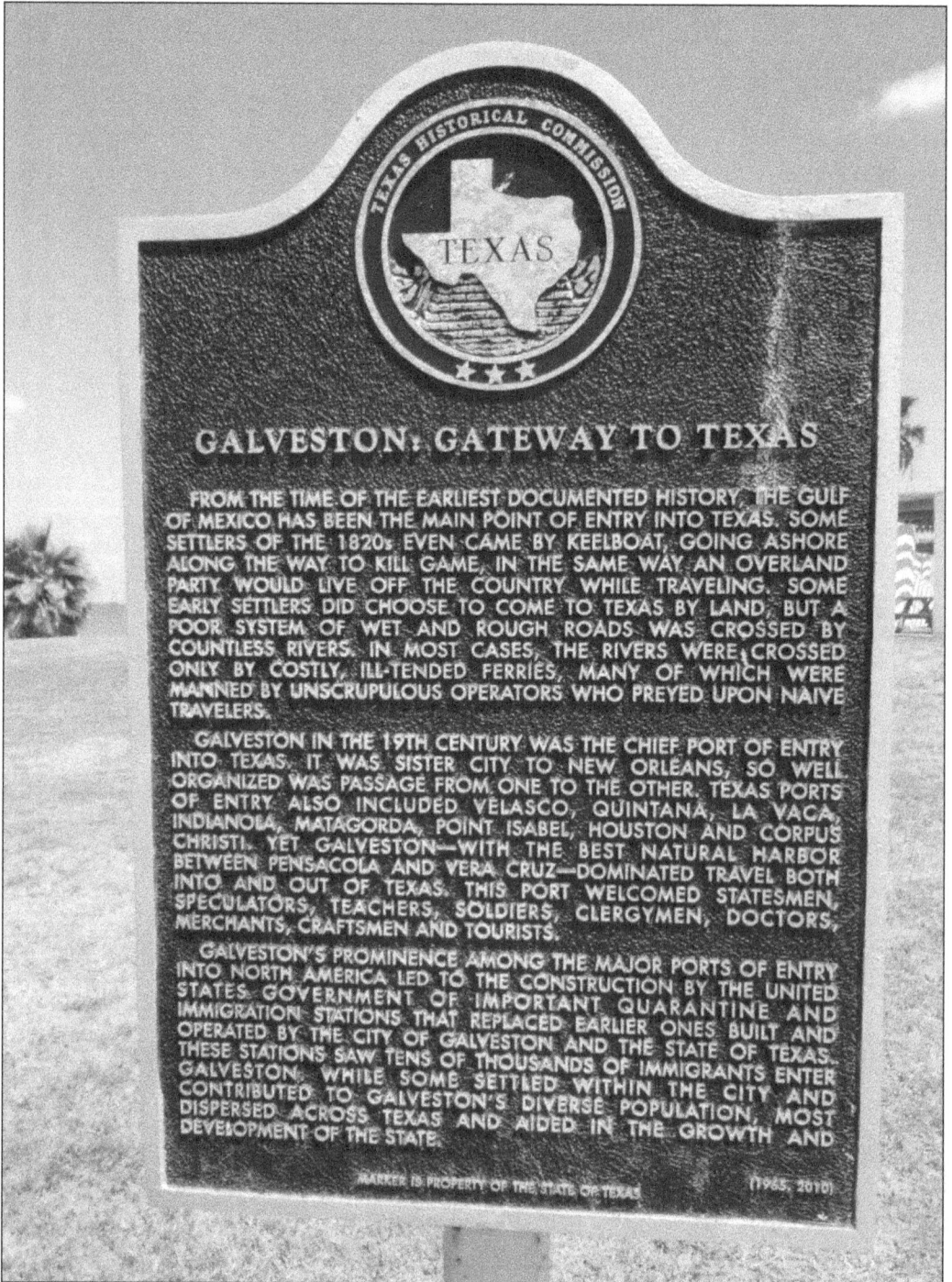

GALVESTON: GATEWAY TO TEXAS

FROM THE TIME OF THE EARLIEST DOCUMENTED HISTORY, THE GULF OF MEXICO HAS BEEN THE MAIN POINT OF ENTRY INTO TEXAS. SOME SETTLERS OF THE 1820s EVEN CAME BY KEELBOAT, GOING ASHORE ALONG THE WAY TO KILL GAME, IN THE SAME WAY AN OVERLAND PARTY WOULD LIVE OFF THE COUNTRY WHILE TRAVELING. SOME EARLY SETTLERS DID CHOOSE TO COME TO TEXAS BY LAND, BUT A POOR SYSTEM OF WET AND ROUGH ROADS WAS CROSSED BY COUNTLESS RIVERS. IN MOST CASES, THE RIVERS WERE CROSSED ONLY BY COSTLY, ILL-TENDED FERRIES, MANY OF WHICH WERE MANNED BY UNSCRUPULOUS OPERATORS WHO PREYED UPON NAIVE TRAVELERS.

GALVESTON IN THE 19TH CENTURY WAS THE CHIEF PORT OF ENTRY INTO TEXAS. IT WAS SISTER CITY TO NEW ORLEANS, SO WELL ORGANIZED WAS PASSAGE FROM ONE TO THE OTHER. TEXAS PORTS OF ENTRY ALSO INCLUDED VELASCO, QUINTANA, LA VACA, INDIANOLA, MATAGORDA, POINT ISABEL, HOUSTON AND CORPUS CHRISTI. YET GALVESTON—WITH THE BEST NATURAL HARBOR BETWEEN PENSACOLA AND VERA CRUZ—DOMINATED TRAVEL BOTH INTO AND OUT OF TEXAS. THIS PORT WELCOMED STATESMEN, SPECULATORS, TEACHERS, SOLDIERS, CLERGYMEN, DOCTORS, MERCHANTS, CRAFTSMEN AND TOURISTS.

GALVESTON'S PROMINENCE AMONG THE MAJOR PORTS OF ENTRY INTO NORTH AMERICA LED TO THE CONSTRUCTION BY THE UNITED STATES GOVERNMENT OF IMPORTANT QUARANTINE AND IMMIGRATION STATIONS THAT REPLACED EARLIER ONES BUILT AND OPERATED BY THE CITY OF GALVESTON AND THE STATE OF TEXAS. THESE STATIONS SAW TENS OF THOUSANDS OF IMMIGRANTS ENTER GALVESTON. WHILE SOME SETTLED WITHIN THE CITY AND CONTRIBUTED TO GALVESTON'S DIVERSE POPULATION, MOST DISPERSED ACROSS TEXAS AND AIDED IN THE GROWTH AND DEVELOPMENT OF THE STATE.

MARKER IS PROPERTY OF THE STATE OF TEXAS   (1965, 2010)

For decades, Galveston had been a prominent entry point into the United States. Pelican Island was a major quarantine and immigration station before and after the Civil War. Multitudes of immigrants coming into the United States brought the real threat of yellow fever and other diseases. (AF.)

Pictured are "quaker guns" (logs used as ruses to imitate cannons) in Confederate fortifications in Manassas Junction in March 1862. Confederates also placed quakers on Pelican Island to delay Union naval attacks. Regardless, Comdr. William Renshaw led Union forces in overtaking Galveston in October 1862. (LOC.)

The Great Hurricane of September 1900, with winds up to 135 mph, devastated Galveston Island as well as the early immigration and quarantine facilities on Pelican Island. Pictured is a stereoscopic photograph of debris tossed across Galveston Bay near Texas City. (LOC.)

GALVESTON QUARANTINE STATIONS

UNREGULATED ENTRY OF IMMIGRANTS THROUGH THE PORT OF GALVESTON IN THE LATE 1830s GREATLY CONTRIBUTED TO LOCAL OUTBREAKS OF YELLOW FEVER AND OTHER COMMUNICABLE DISEASES. THE YOUNG CITY INSTITUTED QUARANTINE MEASURES IN 1839 AND IN 1853 BUILT TEXAS' FIRST QUARANTINE STATION ON THE EASTERN TIP OF GALVESTON ISLAND. YELLOW FEVER RETURNED TO PLAGUE THE COMMUNITY IN 1867 AND 1868.

A LARGER QUARANTINE STATION, BUILT BY THE CITY IN 1870, WAS DESTROYED BY HURRICANE WINDS IN 1875. THE STATE BUILT NEW FACILITIES IN 1879 AND AGAIN IN 1885 AT A SITE IN GALVESTON KNOWN AS FORT POINT. SHIPS SUSPECTED OF HARBORING INFECTED CREW, PASSENGERS, OR CARGO WERE NOT ALLOWED TO ENTER GALVESTON'S PORT. A NEW STATION, BUILT ON NEARBY PELICAN ISLAND BY THE STATE IN 1892, WAS DESTROYED IN THE STORM OF 1900. TEXAS BUILT ITS LAST QUARANTINE STATION AT THE FORT POINT SITE IN 1902. THIS STATION MERGED WITH FEDERAL OPERATIONS IN 1919.

A FEDERALLY FUNDED 10-STRUCTURE QUARANTINE FACILITY, SECURED WITH THE HELP OF GALVESTON'S FEDERAL LIAISON, COLONEL WALTER GRESHAM, WAS COMPLETED HERE ON PELICAN ISLAND IN 1915. THE STATION WAS NOTED FOR ITS SERENE AND BEAUTIFUL GROUNDS, WHICH INCLUDED OLEANDERS, PALMS AND BERMUDA GRASS. HOWEVER, THE PARK-LIKE ATMOSPHERE DID NOT INTERFERE WITH THE STATION'S PURPOSE OF INSPECTING SHIPS BOUND NOT ONLY FOR GALVESTON BUT FOR HOUSTON AND OTHER GALVESTON BAY PORTS. PELICAN ISLAND FEDERAL QUARANTINE STATION, WHICH CLOSED IN 1950, INSPECTED AN ESTIMATED 30,000 SHIPS THAT BROUGHT AN ESTIMATED 750,000 IMMIGRANTS TO TEXAS DURING ITS 35 YEARS OF OPERATION.

(1993)

MARKER IS PROPERTY OF THE STATE OF TEXAS

The early 1900s found Galveston rebuilding, including a new, larger quarantine facility on Pelican Island. Over 750,000 immigrants passed through Galveston to the mainland in 35 years, going into the post–World War II era. In 1965, Galveston philanthropist and Texas A&M graduate George Mitchell purchased and donated land on Pelican Island to build Texas A&M University at Galveston. (AF.)

After World War II, USS *Cavalla* was to be sold as scrap metal. The US Submarine Veterans of World War II had an agreement with the Navy to gain possession of another submarine, USS *Cabrilla*, but it was deteriorating. Instead, the *Cabrilla* was scrapped and *Cavalla*, the "Lucky Lady," was towed to Galveston. She was dry-berthed on Pelican Island as a newly commissioned vessel in the Texas Navy. (AUWC.)

In the 1970s, Seawolf Park was bookended by the ships and the Seawolf Park pavilion and pier. The pavilion was built to host meetings, weddings, and conferences, but in 2008, Hurricane Ike laid havoc to the structure, rendering it unusable. The pier at the lower end of the photograph would become a favored fishing spot during flounder or sand trout seasons. (USNHHC.)

Pictured is the entrance gate to Seawolf Park in August 2001. From its inception and for the next two decades, Seawolf Park existed as a nice fishing spot with an adjoining, quaint Navy museum. Indifference and neglect allowed the USS *Cavalla*, USS *Stewart*, and other artifacts and structures to decay. (AUWC.)

USS *Cavalla* in the early days had two ramps for boarding, and prior to Hurricane Ike in 2008, she sat low into the ground where her berthing cradle was located. In later photographs, *Cavalla* sits higher on the ground. She rose during the storm, allowing dirt to fill in under her. (AUWC.)

Annual commemorative military ceremonies began soon after the naval museum opened its gates (or hatches) in the mid-1970s. Ceremonies honoring veterans on November 11, fallen servicemembers on Memorial Day, and crew reunions became a Galveston way of life, bringing World War II veterans and local military and civic leaders to Pelican Island. (AUWC.)

Pictured is a framed copy of the Mayor of Galveston's proclamation that April 7–13, 1975, was to be honored as Submarine Week. Mayor Ralph A. Apffel urged "each and every citizen to be aware of the outstanding contributions of the Submarine Service to the security of this Nation in time of war, and as an effective guardian of peace." (AUWC.)

The World War I concrete tanker SS *Selma* lies just off the northeast end of Seawolf Park. The largest of her kind, *Selma* was constructed to save steel for the war effort. She was damaged near Mexico in 1920, and attempted repairs back in Galveston proved fruitless. *Selma* was scuttled to make a fishing pier and continues to be a study in concrete naval design and a source of visitor questions. (Photograph by Christy Gossett.)

Nearby Bolivar beach homes were struck hard by Hurricane Ike in 2008. Ike, like many major storms that hit the Gulf Coast, caused a lot of damage to Galveston County, including Seawolf Park. It helped gain attention to the situation on the island. (LOC.)

Hurricane Ike caused significant damage across Seawolf Park due to its powerful surge. It damaged the pavilion and pushed USS *Stewart* over onto its starboard side. Fortunately for *Stewart*, a smaller fishing boat was washed up under her, cushioning her fall. *Stewart* only sustained some hull damage and interior flooding. The other boat was not so lucky. (AUWC.)

USS *Cavalla* was also affected by Ike's surging waters. She rose up off her berthing cradle three to four feet and "cruised" the park for 10 feet before resettling near her original berth. Local Navy veterans who had served on *Cavalla* joked it was a sight "for those who thought they would never see *Cavalla* water borne." (AUWC.)

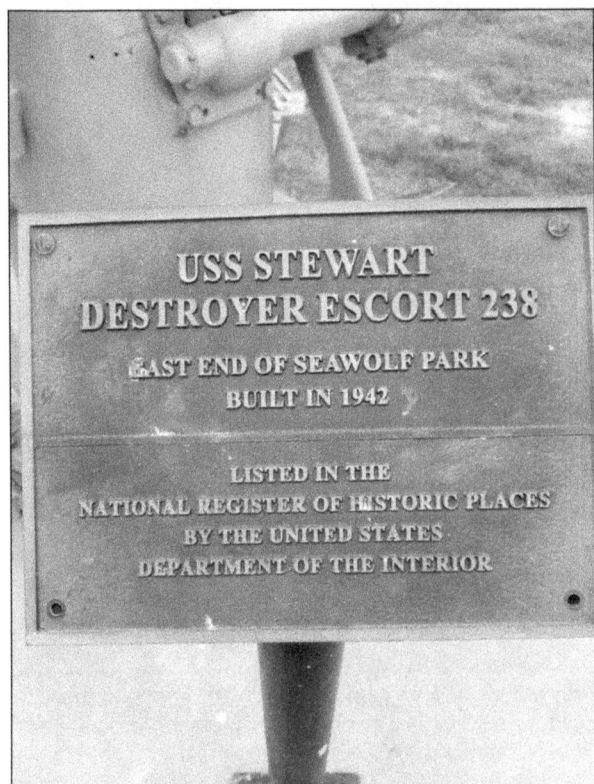

USS STEWART
DESTROYER ESCORT 238

EAST END OF SEAWOLF PARK
BUILT IN 1942

LISTED IN THE
NATIONAL REGISTER OF HISTORIC PLACES
BY THE UNITED STATES
DEPARTMENT OF THE INTERIOR

As time passed, changes occurred at Seawolf Park. The fighter jet made way for a personnel carrier, then some torpedoes. The bamboo hutches were reduced to only a few, and a memorial plaza, complete with a compass rose, was installed between the vessels. Some signage commemorating lost submarines and their crews was also put in place. (AUWC.)

Throughout the 1980s to the early 2000s, artifacts and displays began to appear at the naval museum that significantly added to its public appeal as a location to enjoy and further interest in World War II history. The sail of the USS *Tautog*, the conning tower of the USS *Carp*, and two three-inch guns from the battleship *Texas* all made their way to Seawolf Park. (KC.)

Pictured is the sail of the Sturgeon-class attack submarine USS *Tautog* (SSN-639), saved from the Ship and Submarine Recycling Program (also known as scrapping) and donated to Seawolf Park by her former skippers in 2006. The other artifact is the substructure conning tower compartment, complete with periscope, from the Balao-class World War II submarine USS *Carp* (SS-338). (KC.)

Pictured is the patch of USS *Tautog*. Honoring her World War II namesake, Tambor-class submarine USS *Tautog* (SS-199), the patch depicts a shadow of the past *Tautog* inside the newer nuclear submarine, which was in fact large enough to hold a World War II submarine. (USNHHC.)

During her fourth war patrol in the Pacific, the World War II–era USS *Tautog* conducted some recruiting while at war. She found a fishing schooner with a mixed crew of Japanese and Filipino sailors and fired a few shells across the schooner's bow. The Filipinos quickly dove overboard and swam to the *Tautog*, later enlisting in the US Navy. (USNHHC.)

In 1999, the US Navy re-donated USS *Cavalla* and *Stewart* to the nonprofit Cavalla Historical Foundation and the Galveston Park Board. The naval portion of Seawolf Park was renamed the American Undersea Warfare Center. Just over the drawbridge, this sign points the way down a long road to the end of Pelican Island, where Seawolf Park awaits visitors. (KC.)

This veteran and POW/MIA memorial stone was donated to the naval museum along with flagpoles and a fallen soldier battle cross (soldier's boots, rifle, and helmet). This memorial has been the centerpiece of each annual ceremony honoring veterans over the last half decade. (KC.)

Just across the Galveston Channel sits the US Coast Guard Station Galveston, home of the Coast Guard Cutter *Dauntless* (WMEC-624), a premier "drug buster" with over 85 illegal narcotics busts to her credit, as well as other visiting Coast Guard shipping. The Coast Guard station is strategically placed to protect and defend Galveston shipping entering and exiting Galveston Harbor. (KC.)

Visitors always bring out their inner *Titanic* at the bow of USS *Stewart*. The euphoric feeling expands when a cruise ship passes within hundreds of feet, blasting its tropical paradise music. Carnival, Disney, and Royal Caribbean cruise lines all call Galveston's port home. (KC.)

The mission of the Cavalla Historical Foundation is to restore the vessels from previous degradation due to neglect; preserve the ships for veterans, visitors, and history buffs; and educate all visitors on the actions and sacrifices of the Silent Service and the defenders of the North Atlantic. (KC.)

Members of the Marine Corps League of Galveston provide buglers who play "Taps" each year during Seawolf Park's Memorial Day and Veterans Day ceremonies. One of the buglers, Korean War Marine veteran Guy Taylor (1932–2017), was known as the Marine who played "Taps" each evening, paying tribute to his fellow veterans. (KC.)

Seawolf Park is named in honor of the crew of the USS *Seawolf*, but the submarine inside the fence is USS *Cavalla*. Capt. Ernest "Zeke" Zellmer was on the *Cavalla* as its plotting officer during the sub's historic first patrol. Here, he is speaking at the April 2016 *Cavalla* reunion of former SS-244 and SSN-684 crew members. (DRKC.)

Within earshot of Seawolf Park, fishermen and nature are in a continuous tango as trawlers fight flocking birds, pelicans fly in V-formations like World War II fighter squadrons dive-bombing wading anglers, and the anglers, like a sea of bobbing prairie dogs, vie for their favorite spot as fish pass through the channel to the more open Galveston Bay and Gulf of Mexico. (KC.)

Pictured are the different types of torpedoes used during World War II and postwar periods. These "fish" currently sit within the stern outer doors of USS Cavalla. This angle shows the initial view of the ships upon entering the American Undersea Warfare Center naval museum. The lower port-side torpedo is named "Al's Torpedo" after one of the longtime maintainers who enjoyed painting the Cavalla fish logo. (KC.)

Two

USS SEAWOLF

The World War II Sargo-class USS *Seawolf* (SS-197) was the Pacific Fleet's seventh most lethal submarine, with 18 ships displacing 71,609 tons destroyed. *Seawolf* received two Navy Unit Commendations and 13 Battle Stars over 15 patrols from December 8, 1941, to October 3, 1944. Built in 1938 by the Portsmouth Navy Yard, *Seawolf* was launched in August 1939 and commissioned December 1, 1939, with Lt. Comdr. Frederick Warder in command.

Except for two fewer torpedo tubes, *Seawolf* had otherwise similar dimensions, propulsion, crew complement, and capabilities as Seawolf Park's Gato-class *Cavalla*. *Seawolf* made the most of the tubes she had, as her commanders gained reputations for attacking the enemy and returning to port with no torpedoes. *Seawolf's* crew called their skipper "Fearless Freddy," although never to his face.

Seawolf was crucial in identifying Mark XIV torpedo malfunctions experienced by submariners at the beginning of World War II. The torpedo misfired and ran deep, frustrating attacks and endangering submarines and crews. From April to November 1942, *Seawolf's* skipper experimented with different combat approaches, documented the Mark XIV's deficiencies, and helped make it a reliable weapon, significantly increasing submarine lethality.

On January 10, 1943, *Seawolf* battled a Japanese convoy for 48 hours, getting nine hits and sinking three ships. With three torpedoes left, she found a six-ship convoy. *Seawolf* attacked, then maintained contact, fighting using only her three-inch deck gun until USS *Whale* (SS-239) arrived and joined the battle.

Lt. Comdr. Albert Bontier took *Seawolf* on her 15th war patrol on September 21, 1944. *Seawolf* was carrying 17 Army soldiers led by Capt. Howell S. Kopp toward the Philippines when, near the Maluku Islands, nearby destroyer escort USS *Shelton* was torpedoed by Japanese submarine *Ro-41*. *Shelton's* sister DEs went searching for payback. It is believed that USS *Rowell* (DE-403) detected a submarine. Although the contact was in a safe lane, *Rowell* attacked it and sank it. It was not *Ro-41*, and *Seawolf* no longer responded to recognition signals. On December 28, 1944, *Seawolf* was declared lost and was struck from the Navy Ship Registry in January 1945. Seawolf Park was named to commemorate her sacrifice and to honor her service to the United States.

The memorial sign located on the starboard side of USS *Cavalla* at Seawolf Park honors the 83 submariners and 17 Army soldiers on board the USS *Seawolf* who lost their lives while on patrol in the Pacific during World War II. The officer in charge of the Army squad was Capt. Howell Stewart Kopp. (KC.)

The plaque for USS *Seawolf* is one of 52 commemorating the submarines still on "eternal patrol" after World War II. The plaque lies next to the others in an unending circle inside the Memorial Plaza Compass Rose display at Seawolf Park. (KC.)

This bow view of USS *Seawolf* was taken in the waters off Mare Island Navy Yard, California, in 1943. *Seawolf* was sponsored by Syria F. Kalbfus, wife of Adm. Edward C. Kalbfus, on August 15, 1939. Admiral Kalbfus was a member of the Navy Court of Inquiry into the attack on Pearl Harbor. *Seawolf* made 15 war patrols, seven under the command of Lt. Comdr. Fredrick "Freddy" Warder. Warder was nicknamed "Fearless Freddy" by crew members due to his steadfast calmness during attack positioning and the inevitable depth charges that followed. After his death in 2000 at the age of 95, Warder's daughter Grace told *The Washington Post*, "He knew he wasn't fearless. He was as scared as anybody in battle." After the war, Warder rose to the rank of rear admiral and was awarded the Navy Cross, Bronze Star, and Legion of Merit for outstanding service to the country. At Mare Island, Warder relinquished command to another hard charger, Lt. Comdr. Royce L. Gross, or "Googy," who led *Seawolf* on her eighth through twelfth patrols, when she engaged and damaged or sunk 15 Japanese ships. (USNHHC.)

Mary M. Warder, wife of Rear Adm. "Freddy" Warder, christens the nuclear submarine USS *Thresher* (SSN-593) during launching ceremonies at the Portsmouth Naval Shipyard, Maine, on July 9, 1960. Others present are, from left to right, Mrs. C. Pattisen, Lt. Dale E. Deverspicke (Chaplains Corps), and Capt. Henry P. Rumble. (USNHHC.)

USS *Seawolf* is pictured on May 9, 1944, off Hunters Point, San Francisco. After a major overhaul, *Seawolf* headed to Pearl Harbor with a new skipper, Lt. Comdr. Richard Lynch, and a new mission: She was to photograph a potential Japanese fortification on the Palau Islands in preparation for an Allied attack. (USNHHC.)

Seawolf was stationed at Manila Bay, Philippines, on December 8, 1941 (December 7 in Hawaii), when her Navy family was attacked. Pictured are the battleships USS *Maryland* (BB-46), damaged by two bomb hits, and on the right, USS *Oklahoma* (BB-37), capsized as she sat moored on Battleship Row. (USNHHC.)

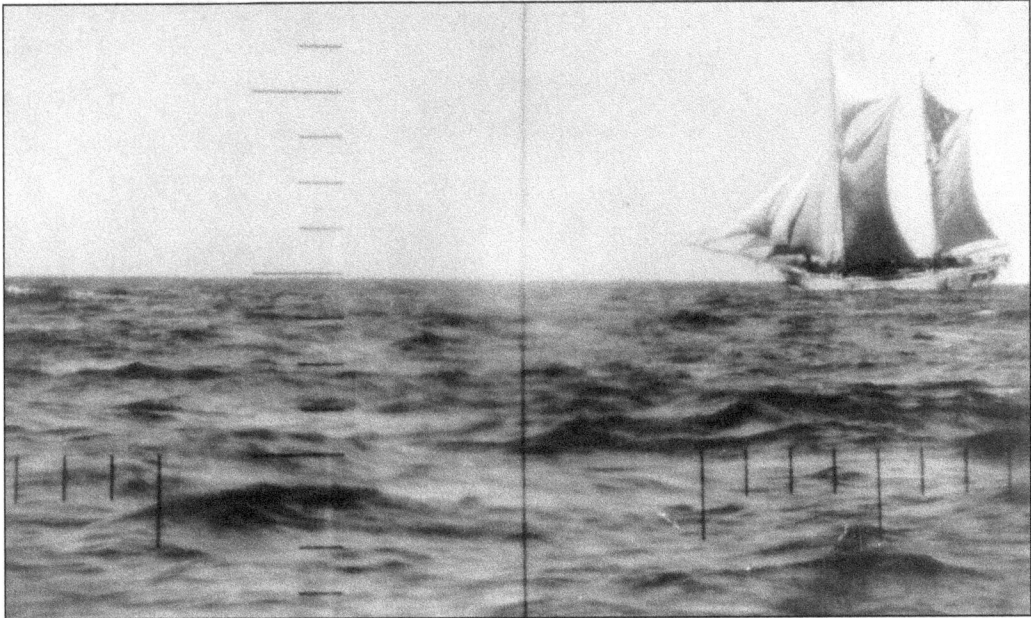

Credited with 18 enemy ships sunk before she herself was lost, USS *Seawolf* was one of the more successful offensive weapons in the Navy's arsenal. Here is a picture from her periscope lining up a 75-ton sailing vessel for destruction. Not knowing who or what each ship carried, every unmarked vessel was considered a possible enemy combatant. (USNHHC.)

USS *Seawolf*'s skippers had reputations for never coming home with a torpedo. Here, *Seawolf* has her eye on Japanese patrol boat No. 39 on April 23, 1943, near Okinawa. She fired her torpedoes and watched as the patrol boat slipped under the surface. (NARA.)

Launched March 15, 1921, patrol boat No. 39 was the former Momi-class Japanese destroyer *Tade*. Eighteen years later, *Tade* and eight of her sister ships were converted and reclassified as patrol boats for escort duty, with reduced power and revamped armaments. Depth charges were added as well as 25mm anti-aircraft guns and landing craft. All but one of these patrol boats were destroyed during the war in the Pacific. (NARA.)

Seawolf's periscope shows her lining up the Japanese cargo ship *Gifu Maru* for a torpedo run near the Philippines on November 2, 1942. Periscope photography was initially used to confirm attack results until USS *Nautilus* (SS-168) performed periscope photography for intelligence collection against the Pacific atoll Apamama on November 19–24, 1943. The name "Maru" used in Japanese civilian shipping meant "circle," or "protector of the (floating) city." (NARA.)

US Navy ships and submarines have several logos and designs to represent their missions and their success. Here is a battle flag depicting a wolf on a torpedo with the USS *Seawolf's* hull number. The hash marks on either side represent *Seawolf's* 18 kills. (AUWC.)

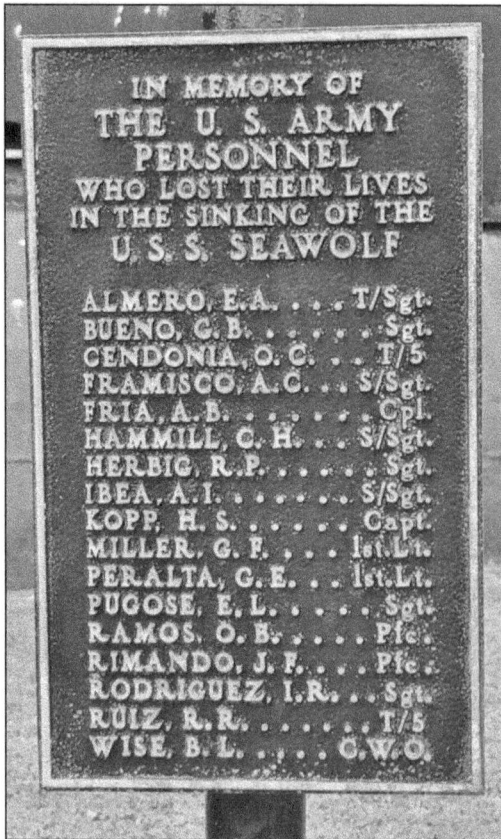

This plaque along Memorial Plaza honors the 17 US Army scouts on eternal patrol with the crew of USS *Seawolf*. Capt. Howell S. Kopp of the 31st Infantry Division ("Old Dixie") was their senior officer. He was quoted as saying, "I feel it is my duty to the Army and my Country to put my abilities to the best use, and experience has proven, I'm a Good Scout." (KC.)

IN MEMORY OF
THE U. S. ARMY PERSONNEL
WHO LOST THEIR LIVES IN THE SINKING OF THE
U. S. S. SEAWOLF

ALMERO, E.A. . . . . T/Sgt.
BUENO, C. B. . . . . . Sgt.
CENDONIA, O. C. . . T/5
FRAMISCO, A.C. . . S/Sgt.
FRIA, A. B. . . . . . . Cpl.
HAMMILL, C. H. . . S/Sgt.
HERBIG, R. P. . . . . . Sgt.
IBEA, A. I. . . . . . . S/Sgt.
KOPP, H. S. . . . . . Capt.
MILLER, G. F. . . . 1st.Lt.
PERALTA, G. E. . . 1st.Lt.
PUGOSE, E. L. . . . . Sgt.
RAMOS, O. B. . . . . Pfc.
RIMANDO, J. F. . . . Pfc.
RODRIGUEZ, I. R. . . Sgt.
RUIZ, R. R. T/5
WISE, B. L. . . . . C.W.O.

This shadow box contains Kopp's Alamo Scout patch and a knife he took from a Japanese soldier in New Guinea. Awarded the Silver Star, Kopp was the first World War II Dixie Division soldier to be decorated. An October 1944 inquiry was held and found USS *Rowell* had sunk *Seawolf. Rowell's* captain, Comdr. Harry Barnard, was censured for making insufficient efforts to identify his target and attacking the *Seawolf*. (Michael Shear.)

Three

USS CAVALLA

USS *Cavalla* (SS-244) was awarded the Presidential Unit Citation for actions on her first patrol near the Philippines from May 31 to August 3, 1944, under the command of Lt. Comdr. Herman J. Kossler (1911–1988). She was also awarded four Battle Stars for operations in the Pacific.

Cavalla was a fleet submarine with a crew of six officers and 54 enlisted. She was long (311 feet, 9 inches) and sleek (27-foot-3-inch beam), displacing 1,550 tons while surfaced. Driven by four 1,600-horsepower General Motors V-16 diesel engines, two 126-cell Sargo battery banks, and four General Electric propulsion motors to drive her two screws, *Cavalla* could reach 21 knots surfaced or 10 knots submerged. War patrols were 60 to 70 days long, usually submerging from 18 to 20 hours at a time. *Cavalla* had a range of over 11,000 nautical miles on the surface at a cruising speed of 10 knots.

Cavalla had ten 21-inch torpedo tubes with a load of 24 Mark-14 or Mark-16 torpedoes. Deck weaponry changed during her time at sea. Commissioned with one 3-inch, 50-caliber gun and four machine guns, Bofors 40mm and Oerlikon 20mm guns were added later.

From 1944 to 1946, *Cavalla* was an attack submarine, sinking over 34,000 tons of enemy shipping, including the Imperial Japanese Navy carrier *Shokaku* during the Battle of the Philippine Seas. After the war, she was decommissioned and placed in the Navy Reserve Fleet in New London, Connecticut. Decommissioned again after a tour with Submarine Squadron 8, the Electric Boat Company converted her into a hunter-killer submarine (SSK-244) on September 3, 1952. *Cavalla* was recommissioned and served with Submarine Squadron 10/Submarine Development Group 2 to experiment with new sonar equipment.

In 1963, *Cavalla* was reclassified as AGSS-244, an auxiliary submarine. On December 30, 1969, *Cavalla* was decommissioned for the final time and struck from the Naval Register list. Unlike many other submarines of her generation, *Cavalla* maintained her Lucky Lady resiliency. On January 21, 1971, USS *Cavalla* became a museum ship at Seawolf Park in Galveston.

U.S. SUBMARINE CAVALLA
DOWN THE WAYS
NOVEMBER 14, 1943
ELECTRIC BOAT CO. GROTON, CONN.

USS *Cavalla* was a Gato-class attack submarine built later in the war, yet made the most of her short time at sea. Her keel was laid down on March 4, 1943, and she did not put to sea until April 11, 1944. With Lt. Comdr. Herman Kossler in command, she departed Pearl Harbor for her first, historic war patrol on May 31, 1944. (AUWC.)

Officers and crew dressed in their "whites," or dress white uniforms, when getting ready to take command of a vessel. Gato-class subs normally had a crew complement of 6 officers and 54 enlisted, but that number fluctuated as men arrived and departed, as well as when subs took on Army personnel moving from island to island. (AUWC.)

Cavalla is pictured under construction at the Electric Boat Company in 1943. The picture on the crane depicts a mackerel fish (*S. cavalla*) biting Adolf Hitler. (USNHHC.)

Crew members waiting to officially board their submarine are pictured in their temporary quarters aboard a houseboat. Bunks three high seemed to be the norm for enlisted berthing compartments. Sailors' opinions differed about which bunk was preferable. Some liked the bottom, so when the vessel was rolling, they would not fall far. Some preferred the top, so they would not have to deal with others using their bunks as ladders. (USNHHC.)

The skipper of the USS *Cavalla*, Lt. Comdr. Herman Kossler (1911–1988), was born in Portsmouth, Virginia, and was a 1934 graduate of the US Naval Academy at Annapolis. Kossler retired a rear admiral after a successful career and tours in World War II, Korea, and Vietnam. He is buried at the Beaufort National Cemetery next to his wife, Ursula. (AUWC.)

Ship and submarine launching ceremonies are momentous occasions, even during war. Pictured are three of the postcards sent out commemorating *Cavalla's* leap day commissioning. The upper-right card depicts her first decommissioning in 1946, and the other two are from crew reunions. Of note are the use of Hitler and Japanese officer characters, as well as the design and prices of the stamps across the years. (AUWC.)

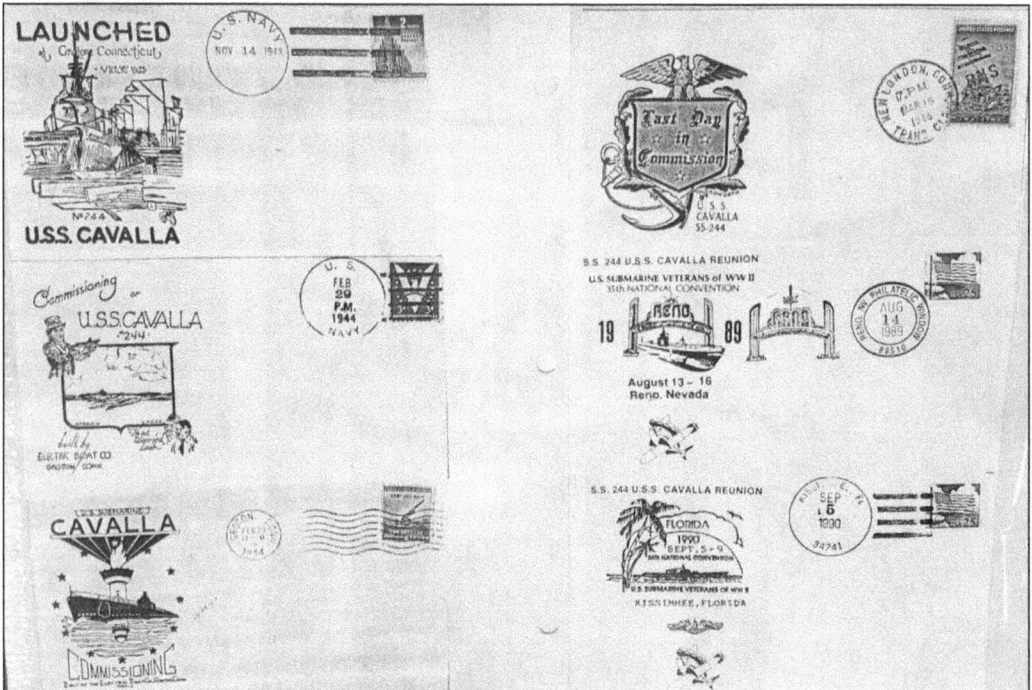

Cavalla's enlisted crew members are pictured here dressed in their service dress blue uniforms. It is said that due to the lack of storage space aboard submarines, crew members folded and stored their service uniforms inside the Naugahyde mattress covers. If they "hot bunked" with another submariner, each would use one side of the mattress. (AUWC.)

With 60 to 80 crewmen on board and cramped duty space like the control room pictured here, *Cavalla* was a crowded submarine. When not on duty, crew stayed in their bunks or spent time in the mess or latrine. Underwater for weeks on end, daily routines and activities to keep sharp were the key to sustained alertness and mission success. (KC.)

Former submariner and Cavalla Historical Foundation president Dr. K.A. Crooks demonstrates how cramped it can get working behind one of the four General Motors V-16 diesel engines. Engine men had to navigate the small spaces behind and below the engines in temperatures that could rise above 100 degrees. (KC.)

Tight quarters and long war patrols under strenuous circumstances created a brotherhood within the crew that was hard to break. Pictured are crew members enjoying a moment topside. Note the beards on several submariners. Uniform and grooming standards were not as stringent out at sea. (CE.)

USS *Cavalla* arrived in Perth, Western Australia, after her second war patrol. On board was the 3-inch, 50-caliber gun capable of firing a 13-pound shell over five miles. (CE.)

The battle flag of USS *Cavalla* was designed by one of the officers on the submarine, Capt. Ernest "Zeke" Zellmer. It has a mackerel fish holding a torpedo "fish" and is surrounded by flags representing ships confirmed sunk by the *Cavalla*. An original of the battle flag can be found on board the ships at Seawolf Park. (KC.)

The large Japanese flag on *Cavalla's* battle flag on the previous page symbolized the most notable of her victories, when she became the only submarine to avenge Pearl Harbor. On June 19, 1944, *Cavalla* found the Imperial Japanese Navy carrier *Shokaku* (pictured here in 1941) recovering planes after a heavy aerial battle near the Marianas Islands. Kossler fired all six forward torpedo tubes, three of which hit their mark. *Shokaku,* one of the carriers involved in the attack on Pearl Harbor, sank in four hours. (USNHHC.)

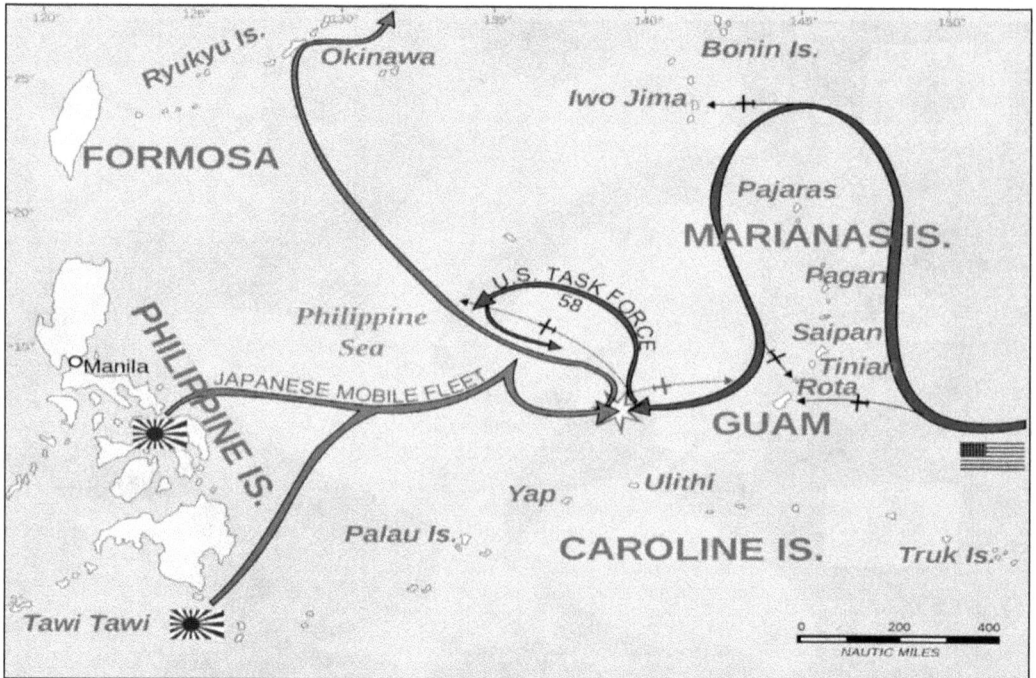

This is a map of the Battle of the Philippine Islands, also known as the Marianas Turkey Shoot. The Imperial Japanese Navy dispatched multiple carrier task forces to Saipan to support their defense of the Marianas Islands. US subs were tasked to find them. *Cavalla* presented the major missing piece of reconnaissance intelligence, which allowed US Naval forces to successfully intercept the Japanese fleet. (LOC.)

A submarine skipper's objective is to find and sink enemy shipping. After allowing the first fleet task force to pass without firing a shot, *Cavalla's* crew was disappointed, to say the least. Lieutenant Commander Kossler was torn between mission orders to "report, not attack" and his gut instinct to sink something. Fortune smiled upon the Lucky Lady when she heard *Shokaku's* screws approaching. The orders were "attack authorized." (CE.)

As *Shokaku* and her escort ships drew near, Kossler and the crew of *Cavalla* made ready their attack. Manning periscopes, plotting courses and attack angles, and preparing fish to be launched, *Cavalla* was ready to hook a big one. Pictured are *Cavalla's* conning tower compartment with periscopes (center) and the targeting data center (right) as they are currently arranged. (KC.)

Plotting for speed

The above may be illustrated graphically:

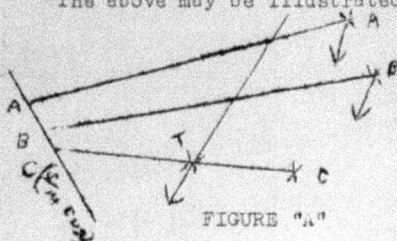

FIGURE "A"

A submarine on course as illustrated sights an enemy ship. At A minutes after sighting an observation is made and plotted. At B minutes and C minutes further observations are made and plotted.

The bearings are accurate, the smallest angle on the bow is probably most accurate and the last and closest range should be the most accurate. Therefore target is at the point T, on course determined by the angle on the bow at first observation.

Draw enemy course line through point T and measure distance run between bearings for speed determination.

On a zigzagging target, the target's course should be indicated at each observation until his track is determined. When two or more observations are made while target is on any one leg, proceed as in the above example for speed determination.

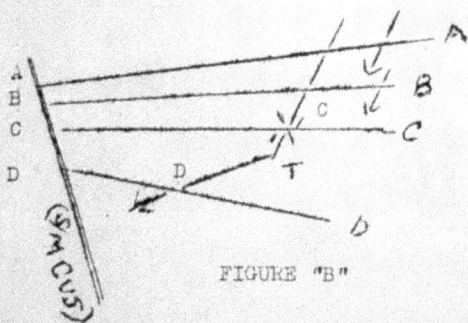

FIGURE "B"

In Figure B, after determining that enemy is on course through point C, another observation places him at pi D. By running his course line back to his previous track (Point T), the plotter can estimate the time of the zig. The speed estimate from C to D is determined by the distances CT + TD.

The plotter should keep the submarine track plotted ahead of the actual position of the submarine to enable him to speed up his work.

It is important that bearing lines be plotted sufficiently long to enable the plotter to quickly shift the enemy track should subsequent observations show a different track than that which has been drawn.

In determining speed, work for a determination of plotted overall speed.

This page from a targeting manual of the 1940s shows the level of plotting that needed to be done in a short time to correctly load targeting data into the torpedoes via the targeting data center. Added to the complexity was the rudimentary communications systems used throughout the submarine and the distance between submarine compartments like the maneuvering room and the control room. It is a wonder that any ships were sunk at all. In sinking the *Shokaku*, Kossler relied on several young officers to plot the best avenue of attack. Officers like Ensign Zeke Zellmer, Lt. (jg) Art Rand, and Lt. Tom Denegre were up to the task. *Cavalla* sank the *Shokaku* using Mark XIV torpedoes. About 13,000 Mark XIVs were built by Naval Torpedo Station Newport, Rhode Island, for World War II anti–surface ship operations. They weighed 1.5 tons, were 20.5 feet long, and contained 600-pound warheads. They ran at speeds up to 46 knots and had an effective firing range in excess of three miles. (AUWC.)

Ens Ed Eeds, Ltjg Art Rand, Ltjg Jim Casler, Mach. Ray Nichols, LCDR Herman Kossler, Lt Tom Denegre, Ens Vance Cathey, Ens Zeke Zellmer

Cavalla officers are pictured at Saipan on July 2, 1944. After a successful mission at the Marianas Islands, Lieutenant Commander Kossler relaxes with his officers. From left to right are Ens. (O1) Ed Eeds, Lt. (jg) (O2) Art Rand, Lt. (jg) (O2) Jim Casler, machinist Ray Nichols, Lieutenant Commander (O5) Kossler, Lt. (O3) Tom Denegre, Ens. (O1) Vance Cathey, and Ens. (O1) Zeke Zellmer. (CE.)

Cavalla's crew was no longer disappointed. They realized that their sub really was the Lucky Lady. They had successfully attacked and sunk the preeminent carrier in the Japanese Navy and, afterward, survived the wrath of the carrier's escort destroyers. After she struck *Shokaku*, *Cavalla* endured three hours of depth charges—106 barrels full of explosives seeking them out in order to crack their hull. (AUWC.)

Ancient Order OF THE Deep

TO all sailors wherever it may be, and to all living things of the sea, Greetings: Know ye, that while serving on the U.S.S. CAVALLA in the Great War of the United Nations against the Axis, there appeared within Our Royal Domains one BURGESS, Jesse D., Mo1M2c, USNR paying his respects to Neptune's Rex, and was found worthy to be a TRUSTY SHELLBACK.

DAVY JONES
HIS MAJESTY'S SCRIBE

NEPTUNUS REX
RULER OF THE RAGING MAIN

The Submarine Combat Insignia

with stars as indicated for completion of 3 successful patrols has been

Awarded to:
BURGESS, Jesse Dodd, Mo1M2c, USNR
on 22 August 1944
by
CAPTAIN, U. S. NAVY

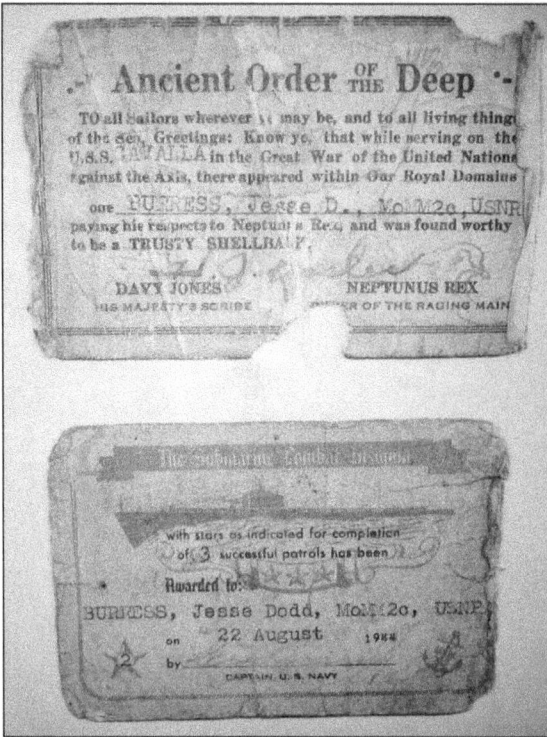

Between war patrols, *Cavalla's* crew found some time for fun and ceremony. The Ancient Order of the Deep ceremony, transforming slimy "Pollywogs" (sailors who had never crossed the equator) into "Trusty Shellbacks" (Sons of Neptune) was one of the more honored traditions. Upon crossing the equator, the more senior Shellbacks would initiate deserving Pollywogs in a ceremony featuring some unusual dress and activities. Crewmen would also be awarded special uniform breast pins after completing successful combat patrols during declared wars. This card for a pin features a side view of a Gato-class submarine with three service stars below, one for each patrol. (AUWC.)

Pictured are senior officers and King Neptune's Trusty Shellbacks initiating Pollywogs into the Ancient Order of the Deep. (CE.)

One of the jobs of a talented crewman was to paint the ship's battle flag on the side of the bridge. It consisted of the sub's emblem and enemy combatant flags representing confirmed victories. In addition to *Shokaku*, *Cavalla* claimed victories in sinking the destroyer *Shimotsuki*, freighters *Kanko Maru* and *Shunsen Maru*, and a small sampan. (CE.)

Here, two crewmen relax in the maneuvering room, looking over a photograph album. Logging their daily lives through a camera lens helped preserve the history of the World War II submarine. (CE.)

During port calls, the crew found opportunities to see the sights—armed, of course, even while in the allied country of Australia. They never knew when a wild kangaroo or dingo might make a surprise attack. (CE.)

The *Cavalla* crew looked for time to relax. Sometimes, it was enough to get on the bridge for some fresh air or take a swim when there was a break in hostilities. Occasionally, sub skippers allowed small mascots on board their submarines to help boost morale. Kossler allowed Lt. T. Denegre to have a dingo pup on board; the puppy's special status was revoked after it urinated in the captain's cabin. (AUWC.)

While on patrol in the South China Sea in 1945, these crewmen knew that if they came under attack, Gato-class submarines could crash dive in less than 30 seconds. *Cavalla* was on its third war patrol off Singapore when she scored her other three major victories. Victories at sea and taking time to relax and reunite with fellow submariners while in port helped get many submariners through the war. (CE.)

Camaraderie was as prevalent as competition to be the best boat in the Pacific. During her fourth patrol, which began February 25, 1945, *Cavalla* patrolled between the Philippines and Singapore. For six weeks, it was uneventful; Allied success in the Pacific was beginning to show. There were no targets to engage, but *Cavalla* did avoid a Japanese air attack as well as an unsuccessful Japanese submarine torpedo run. (AUWC.)

On May 19, 1945, the British T-class submarine HMS *Terrapin* was damaged by depth charges from Japanese convoy escort ships. *Cavalla* found *Terrapin* defenseless and on the surface. Unable to make full speed or dive, *Cavalla* safely escorted *Terrapin* through the Java Sea to Freemantle, Australia, over 2,500 kilometers. Despite making it to port, *Terrapin* was so badly damaged she was decommissioned and later scrapped. (CE.)

Cavalla's final war patrol lasted less than three weeks. On August 15, 1945, the cease fire was sent to all naval vessels. Commander Kossler almost made a fatal error; he stayed on the surface off the coast of Japan to see it up close, but not all Japanese pilots had received the word. A plane dove at *Cavalla*, dropping a bomb that barely missed the sub. (AUWC.)

This view from *Cavalla* shows crews debarking in Tokyo Bay on September 2, 1945, to witness Japanese foreign minister Mamoru Shigemitsu sign Japan's Instrument of Surrender aboard USS *Missouri*. Adm. Chester W. Nimitz invited Adm. Charles Lockwood, commander of submarine forces in the Pacific, to the ceremony and allowed a dozen submarines, including *Cavalla*, to be present in Tokyo Bay alongside the submarine tender USS *Proteus*. (CE.)

The Japanese surrender on the *Missouri* is seen here from a senior naval officer's perspective. Following the ceremony, *Cavalla* headed for home via Guam, Pearl Harbor, the Panama Canal, and up the East Coast to New London, Connecticut. (USNHHC.)

This picture shows the Japanese katana swords surrendered to the Allies led by Gen. Douglas MacArthur. MacArthur ordered the confiscation of all weapons, and many of the swords were thrown into Tokyo Bay, where most of them deteriorated. When told that these weapons were sacred artifacts, MacArthur rescinded his order. (USNHHC.)

off Tokyo
1945

A lookout on USS *Cavalla* sets his sights eastward from Tokyo back home to the United States. The return trip took 34 days and covered a distance of about 11,000 miles. (AUWC.)

After leaving Tokyo, the crew could relax some, but operating a submarine, even in peace time, was still hazardous duty. However, most of the time *Cavalla* rode the surface, allowing more fresh-air time for the crew. (CE.)

Cavalla spent a few days in Guam, giving the crew some rest and relaxation (R&R) time while the sub received some maintenance before coming home. (CE.)

The crew of USS *Cavalla* spent some of their last days together playing baseball and relaxing in Guam in 1945. (AUWC.)

This photograph was taken at Camp Dealy in Guam in 1945. The crew of the *Cavalla* stayed in Quonset huts while waiting for their submarine to return to duty. Quonset huts were named after their origin, Quonset Point, Rhode Island, and were prefabricated buildings formed in a semicircle. They were widely used because they were easy to ship and assemble and were made of galvanized steel. About 160,000 were used during World War II. (CE.)

Captured Japanese Ko-hyoteki midget submarine No. 51 was displayed on Guam in 1945. These mini-subs were about 24 feet long, weighed 46 tons, and had a crew of two. Unlike fleet submarines, mini-subs actually ran faster submerged than on the surface (19 knots versus 6 knots), and each held two torpedoes. No. 19 mini-sub was launched from Japanese submarine I-24 during the attack on Pearl Harbor. (CE.)

The next stop was Pearl Harbor, with memories of the war they just fought and visions of the postwar era beginning. *Cavalla* pulled into port with a view of other submarines as well as USS *Essex* (CV-9), lead ship of the Essex-class carriers. Like *Cavalla*, *Essex* also earned the Presidential Unit Citation and supported the Battle of the Philippine Seas. *Essex* later helped quarantine Cuba in 1962 during the Cuban Missile Crisis. (CE.)

The crew of *Cavalla* visited Hawaii while on R&R. The famous 760-foot volcanic peak with the 350-acre Punchbowl Crater inside was named Diamond Head in the 1700s when it was thought that reflections off crystals in the rocks resembled diamonds. The National Memorial Cemetery of the Pacific (Punchbowl Cemetery) is a national cemetery serving as a memorial to those who served in the US armed forces. (CE.)

Today, it is called the Pali Highway, but in 1945, it was just "the Pali." The road connects Honolulu to the windward side of Oahu and Kaneohe Bay. Known for its breathtaking views and difficult curves, it was a must-see location. (CE.)

Adventurous crew members in their dress white uniforms pose with a native coconut as they prepared to see the sites and try the various tropical foods of Hawaii, like *poi*, a dish made from fermented taro roots. (CE.)

Near the end of Hawaii's pineapple harvest season in 1945, the crew of the *Cavalla* arrived in time to watch pineapples being harvested at a local plantation. Normally, harvest season ran from June through September. (CE.)

Among the sights crewmen desired to see after a long tour in the Pacific were the local hula dancers. Hula is a traditional dance natives used to tell stories, keep history, and preserve mythology and culture. (CE.)

At Pearl Harbor, submarines line up at the docks waiting for maintenance, resupply, and crew rest. Among the line of American flags flying, one flag is possibly French. (CE.)

Of course, while others visited the sights of Oahu, someone had to watch the ship. With his sidearm on his hip and dressed in his bucket hat and dungarees, this crewman scans the docks at Pearl Harbor in 1945. (CE.)

One of the views from *Cavalla's* deck could have been of the 1945 version of graffiti. Note the drawings of a turtle in a bucket hat and early Tom and Jerry cartoon characters on the hand cart. (CE.)

As crew returned from shore leave, they hung around the submarine. Pictured are two submariners sitting atop the 3-inch, 50-caliber gun on deck. One would surmise that if an officer walked by, he might say, "If you're gonna sit on it, might as well paint it!" (CE.)

While about to get underway, Commander Kossler listens as the crew of USS *Cavalla* receive their orders. To get to their home port, *Cavalla* had to wait its turn passing through the Panama Canal locks in 1945. (CE.)

Portsmouth, Virginia, was *Cavalla's* first official US port of call after the war in 1945. Hawaii did not become the Aloha State until August 1959. (CE.)

Coming back from the tropics in the autumn could get chilly as crew onboard *Cavalla* wore a variety of jackets. Note the bow plane folded up along the starboard side, not completely retracted, and the positioning of the anchor. (AUWC.)

At their first US stop, the public came aboard this heroic vessel. The men were happy to be home with family, friends, and some pets. By 1945, the United States had over 260 submarines conducting operations in the Pacific, losing 52 due to all causes. Of the 30,000 sailors assigned to submarines, 16,000 made war patrols. Of those, 3,484 lost their lives (348 officers and 3,136 enlisted). (AUWC.)

In Portsmouth, *Cavalla* overlooked the Salmon-class USS *Skipjack* (SS-184). Commissioned in 1938, *Skipjack* was being repaired in the Philippines when the Japanese attacked Pearl Harbor. She received seven battle stars for her World War II patrol victories and was a target at Bikini Atoll during the July 1946 atomic bomb test. (AUWC.)

Cavalla is pictured in port at Portsmouth, where someone still had to provide security deck side. The Colt M1911 .45-caliber handgun was the service pistol of choice during World War II. It was a single-action, semiautomatic weapon with a seven-round clip. (CE.)

Submariner Chip "Bus" Engler, on board Cavalla in Portsmouth, had to keep the submarine in "ship-shape." The term means "in seamanlike order," from the British demand for their ships to be maintained in excellent order. (CE.)

Each returning ship was met by a US Navy welcoming committee. *Cavalla* received hers at Portsmouth on October 6, 1945. Commander Kossler, skipper of *Cavalla* for its entire wartime duty, greets senior Navy officers as they in turn greet the crew of *Cavalla*. Note the brace for the three-inch gun at left, keeping it in place and steady. Also, note the unusual Navy service dress uniforms worn by the senior officers. These were the short-lived service dress gray uniforms of the mid- to late 1940s. Adm. Ernest King, chief of naval operations, wanted something different than the "land style" of the khaki-colored service dress uniform. The gray style included black buttons, gray shirt, and gray shoulder boards with black stripes. It was said that Admiral Nimitz did not agree with this uniform change and discouraged the wearing of it for Pacific forces. (AUWC.)

Cavalla pulled into New London, Connecticut, on October 6, 1945, where she remained in inactive service until she was decommissioned (the first time) on March 16, 1946. For the next five years, *Cavalla* remained in a "waiting for disposition" status. Was she still useful or was she to be scrapped? Was there luck left in the Lucky Lady? (CE.)

Cabin Grill in New London seemed to be the place to go for the men on October 22, 1945. Notice the submariner on the left (identified as "Bob") wears embroidered dolphins on his sleeve and is wearing his Presidential Unit Citation ribbon (upper-left ribbon with three horizontal stripes) on his chest. (CE.)

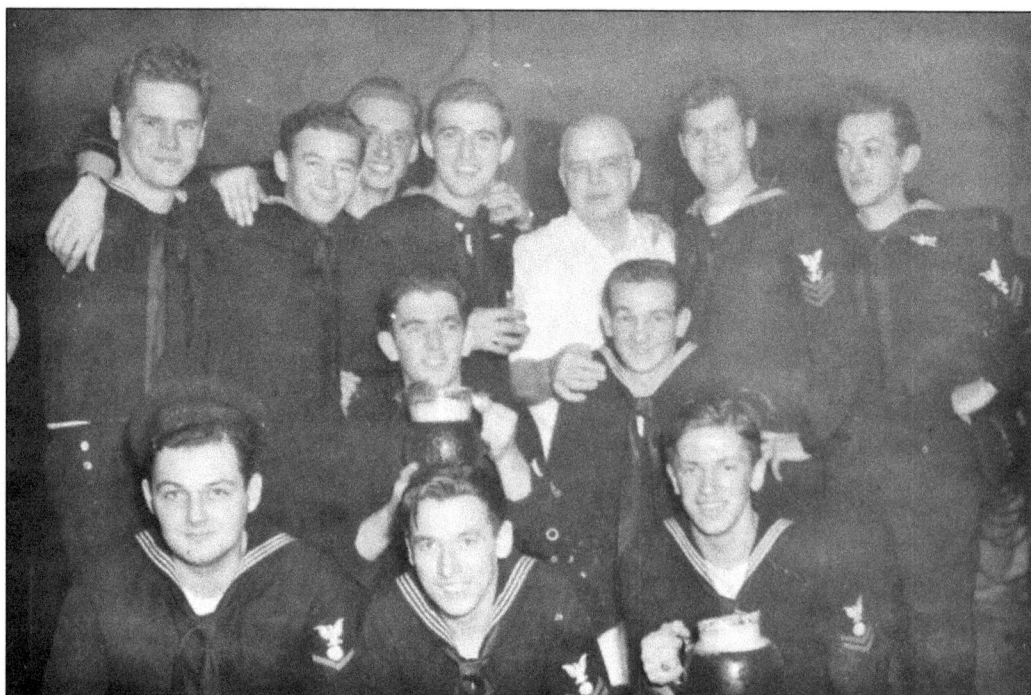

Someone in the crew always knew of a place to go, like the Yellow Dog Club, pictured here in early 1946. Crew members began to be reassigned or discharged as *Cavalla* moved closer to decommissioning. (CE.)

Pictured are photographs of *Cavalla* as a World War II attack submarine (SS-244, top) and a hunter-killer submarine (SSK-244, bottom). Hunter-killers were specifically configured to find, attack, and sink opposing submarines. Key differences included a new bridge, no deck guns, and a more rounded bow. (AUWC.)

This plaque at Seawolf Park shows the skippers of USS *Cavalla* from 1944 to 1968. Commander Kossler led *Cavalla* through World War II and turned her over to a series of commanders during *Cavalla's* reconfigurations from anti-surface warfare, to hunter-killer submarine, to auxiliary (experimental) submarine, until her final decommissioning on June 3, 1968. (AUWC.)

USS CAVALLA SS-244, SSK-244
COMMANDING OFFICERS

CDR H.J. KOSSLER	FEB 44-JAN 46
LCDR E.R. EBERLE	JAN 46-MAR 46
Out of commission	
LCDR M.C. DUNCAN	APR 51-JUL 52
Out of commission	
LCDR W.R. BANKS	JUL 53-JUL 55
LCDR W.S. DELANEY	JUL 55-SEP 56
LCDR G.M. HAYES	SEP 56-DEC 57
LCDR L.F. FITCH	DEC 57-DEC 59
LCDR R.Y. KAUFMAN	DEC 59-MAR 61
LCDR W.J. KRAUS	MAR 61-MAR 63
LCDR E.E. WILLIAMS	MAR 63-MAR 65
LCDR W.F. SMITH	MAR 65-JUN 67
LCDR J.R. BAUMAN	JUN 67-JUN 68
Decommissioned	

This view of *Cavalla* (SSK-244) in September 1953 shows her wider, curved-bow section configured for new passive attack sonar. To accommodate the new sonar equipment, two forward torpedo tubes were removed, and the bridge and sail were remodeled. Placing the sonar so far forward allowed optimum target detection with less internal noise interference. (AUWC.)

This view of the current *Cavalla* forward engine room shows the removal of her No. 2 diesel engine, leaving her with three. In its place, the Navy placed the air-conditioning plant that was moved to make way for more sonar equipment under the control room. (KC.)

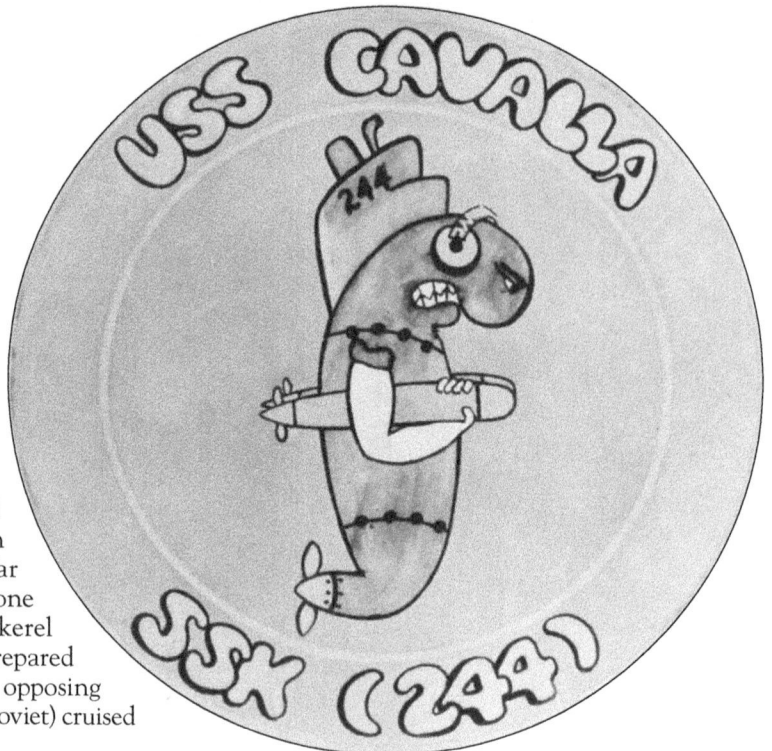

This patch was designed to show *Cavalla*'s mission change from World War II attack submarine to one of passive listener (mackerel with headphones on), prepared to sit, wait, and listen as opposing submarines (presumably Soviet) cruised by. (AUWC.)

Season's Greetings

USS CAVALLA

During the 1950s, skippers of USS *Cavalla* sent out different Christmas cards each year. On this page are two such cards showing slightly different configurations of the submarine. While most pictures show *Cavalla* as being all black, the below image is from a period when she was two-toned. This configuration is closest to what is presented at Seawolf Park today. Note the external hatch opened on the starboard side of the bridge. (Both, AUWC.)

Greetings

USS CAVALLA

Pictured are a series of USS *Cavalla* patches depicting SS-244, SSK-244, and AGSS-244, as well as the nuclear submarine USS *Cavalla* (SSN-684), the Cavalla Historical Foundation, and Seawolf Park. *Cavalla* was donated to the Texas Submarine Veterans of World War II on January 21, 1971, and sent to Seawolf Park shortly thereafter. (AUWC.)

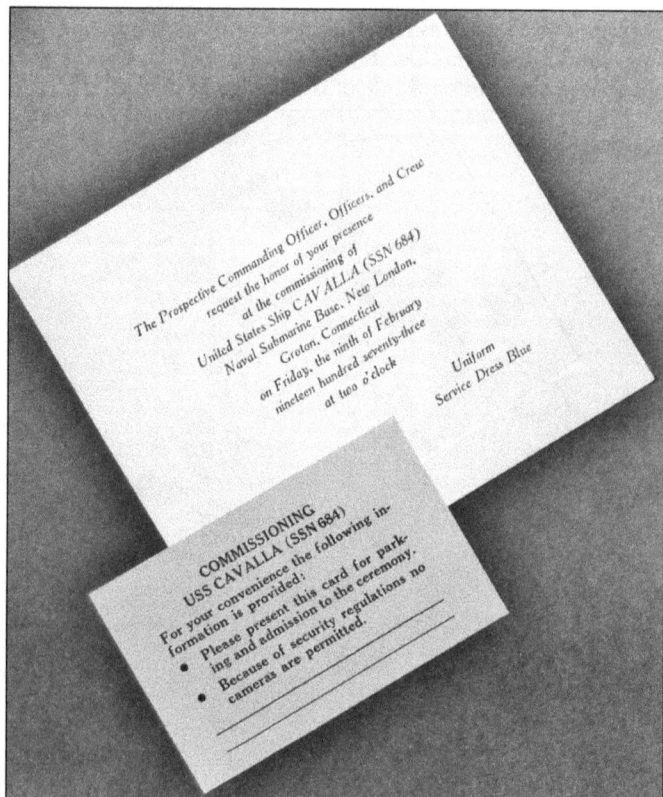

This is the commissioning invitation for a second USS *Cavalla* (SSN-684), a nuclear submarine. Commissioned on February 9, 1973, she joined the Navy nearly 29 years after SS-244 and was birthed from the same location: New London, Connecticut. SSN-684 was decommissioned on March 30, 1998, and was sent to scrap on November 17, 2000, while the Lucky Lady (SS-244) continues on as a memorial naval museum to this day. (AUWC.)

Four

USS STEWART

The Edsall-class USS *Stewart* (DE-238) is one of only two preserved World War II–era US destroyer escorts in the United States today. The other is the USS *Slater* (DE-766), a Cannon-class destroyer-escort still afloat in Albany, New York. Destroyer escorts were built to effectively protect convoys. They were highly maneuverable (*Stewart* could turn in a circle with a diameter only 2.5 times its length of 306 feet!), could travel at speeds up to 21 knots, and could conduct long range operations (9,000 nautical miles at a standard 12 knot speed). At her decommissioning, *Stewart*'s weaponry consisted of three 3-inch, 50-caliber guns, eight 40mm anti-aircraft guns, ten 20mm anti-aircraft guns, two depth charge roll-off tracks astern, eight depth charge (MK-6) projectors (also known as "K-Guns"), and one 24–depth charge Hedgehog system. *Stewart*'s three-foot, 21-inch torpedo tubes were replaced by 40mm guns. Of the 209 sailors aboard, over half were there to man the many weapons at her disposal.

Brown Shipbuilding built *Stewart* in Houston in mid-1942, launching her on November 22. She was commissioned on May 31, 1943, with Lt. Comdr. B.C. Turner in command. At 306 feet long, with a beam of 36 feet, and displacing 1,250 tons empty, *Stewart* was lean, mean, and ready for battle.

USS *Stewart* held an important footnote in history. In October 1943, she reported to the Washington Naval Yard. There, she was ordered to start removing bunks and piping to make way for a special group as tons of filing cabinets and carpeting bearing the seal of the president of the United States came aboard. *Stewart*, with many flag officers and their busy staffs aboard, then cruised down the Potomac, escorting and protecting the presidential yacht of Pres. Franklin D. Roosevelt. Meeting with USS *Iowa* in Chesapeake Bay, the president, his staff, and the military staffs on board all relocated to the much larger *Iowa*. *Stewart* then patrolled ahead of the presidential convoy under the guise of recording pitch and roll observations. The president and his convoy sailed on to Tehran, Iran, to meet Winston Churchill and Joseph Stalin.

Named for Adm. Charles Stewart of War of 1812 fame, USS *Stewart* was built like her sister destroyer escorts because the Allies were losing the North Atlantic convoy battle against the German U-boat wolf packs. Using the Lend Lease Act of March 1941, the United States sold warships and munitions to the British to help their war effort. One need was to have an open-ocean, anti-submarine convoy escort that could maneuver around the convoy and defend it against wolf packs. When the US entered the war, destroyer escorts coming off the assembly line bound for Great Britain instead became US Navy assets. Of the nearly 600 DEs built, about 100 of them were transferred to allies. DEs were classified as major combat vessels, and in the North Atlantic where USS *Stewart* patrolled, their missions were to protect convoys and team up to form hunter-killer task forces in search of submarines. They even performed mail-carrier duties to fleet units. (AUWC.)

A US Navy cargo ship rides the heavy swells while steaming toward the European theater of operations during World War II. Before destroyer escorts became a common sight among North Atlantic trade convoys in late 1943, U-boats sank or damaged 182 ships in 1942 and 155 in 1943, but only 9 in 1944 and 9 again in 1945 prior to VE Day. (USNHHC.)

The destroyer escort maintained an array of weaponry for use against enemy submarines as well as aircraft. With three 3-inch guns, depth charges that could be rolled off the stern or blasted out from the sides, even more deadly Hedgehog depth charges, and an assortment of 40mm and 20mm guns, USS *Stewart* and her siblings were effective at their missions. (KC.)

Here is Comdr. Charles Stewart of the famed battle between his US frigate *Constitution* and defeated British ships HMS *Levant* and HMS *Cyane* the day after the War of 1812 was declared ended. *Constitution* was nicknamed "Old Ironsides" because enemies believed her oak hull was impenetrable to cannon fire. (LOC.)

The frigate *Constitution*, the oldest commissioned ship in the US Navy, was built in 1797 and remains in Boston Harbor to this day with actual US Navy sailors on board. The *Constitution*, like USS *Stewart,* is still serving the country as a memorial to America's past warfighters. (BT.)

USS *Stewart* (DD-224), the second ship named for Admiral Stewart, served from 1920 until March 1942 when it was scuttled at Java in the Pacific when Japanese forces were attacking. The Japanese subsequently raised the ship and recommissioned it into the Japanese navy as patrol boat No. 102. The US Navy recaptured *Stewart* and towed her back to port, but she was too damaged to be useful. *Stewart* was used for target practice and sunk in May 1946. (USNHHC.)

USS *Stewart* (DD-224) is pictured in port in China with four other destroyers. While she served as a Japanese patrol boat, *Stewart* (P-102) was with the Japanese task force that sank USS *Cavalla's* sister Gato-class submarine USS *Harder* (SS-257) with all hands on board. (USNHHC.)

USS *Stewart* had a complement of 8 officers and 201 enlisted men. Often, men seemed to swarm the decks with orchestrated activity. Duty in the North Atlantic conducting convoy escort support was not glamorous—it was treacherous. One crewman described their duty onboard as "seek and destroy missions" against German submarine wolf packs. (USNHHC.)

The crew of the USS *Stewart* party with loved ones between voyages to Naples, Italy. This ship service party took place at the Hotel Edison in New York City in October 2, 1944. The couple in the far back kissing was Chief Gunner's Mate Ralph "Gunner" Meier and Ruth. They waited almost four years to get married. It seems World War II and *Stewart's* frequent assignments kept them apart until they finally married on March 2, 1945. (RS.)

U.S.S. STEWART (DE 238)
VESSEL ON WAYS (BOW VIEW)
BROWN SHIPBUILDING COMPANY
HOUSTON, TEXAS
DE-1 22 - NOVEMBER - 1942

The next few pages show the launching of USS *Stewart* on November 22, 1942, by Brown Shipbuilding of Houston. Pictured here is a bow view of *Stewart* on the ways. (USNHHC.)

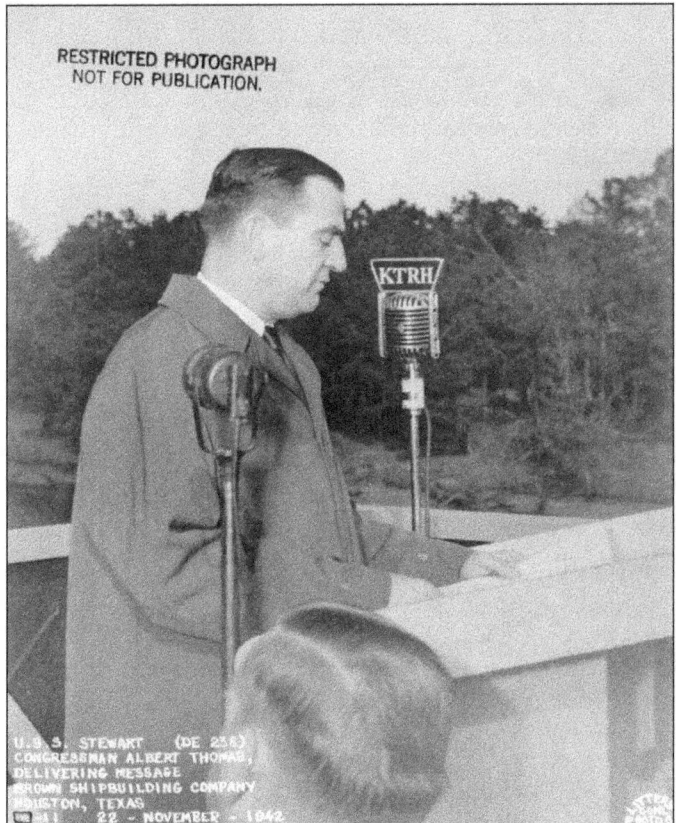

RESTRICTED PHOTOGRAPH
NOT FOR PUBLICATION.

U.S.S. STEWART (DE 238)
CONGRESSMAN ALBERT THOMAS,
DELIVERING MESSAGE
BROWN SHIPBUILDING COMPANY
HOUSTON, TEXAS
DE-1 22 - NOVEMBER - 1942

Congressman Albert Thomas gave an address to the gathered audience at the launching ceremony of USS *Stewart*. (USNHHC.)

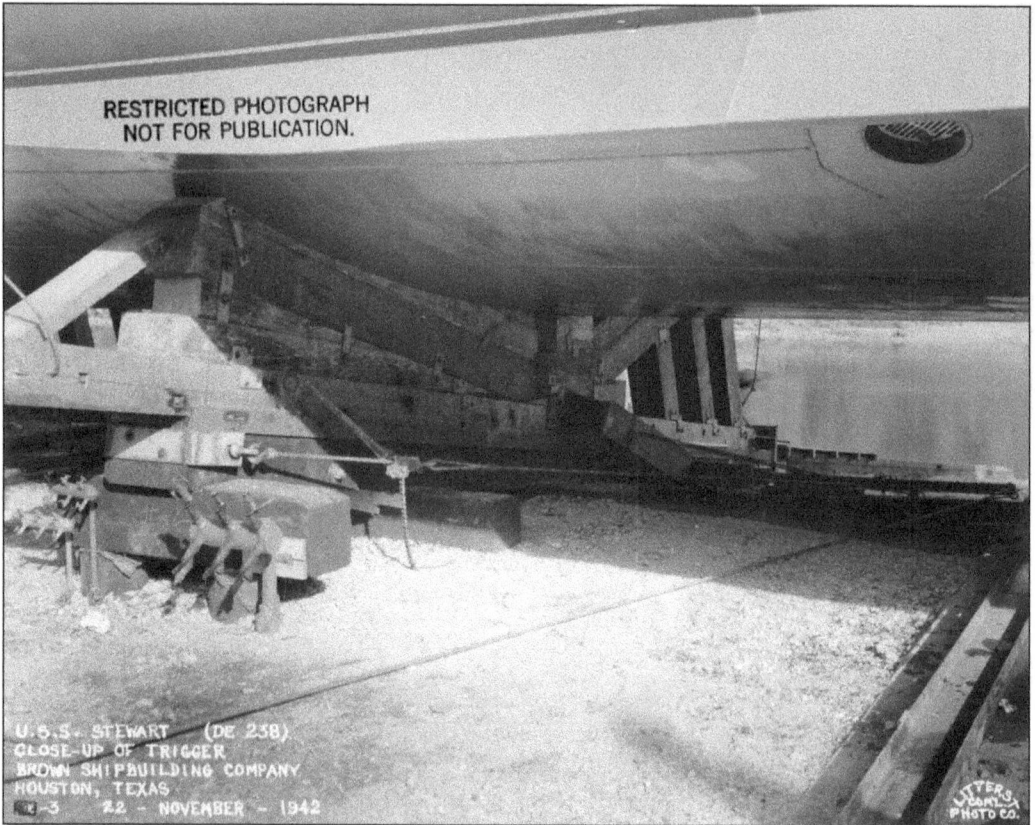

This is a close-up view of the mechanism to trigger the launching of USS *Stewart* into the water. (USNHHC.)

The starting ram's job was to trigger the launch of USS *Stewart* down the ways into the water. (USNHHC.)

Mrs. William A. Porteous Jr. was the sponsor of the launching of USS *Stewart*. (USNHHC.)

RESTRICTED PHOTOGRAPH
NOT FOR PUBLICATION.

U.S.S. STEWART (DE 238)
CHRISTENING OF VESSEL
BROWN SHIPBUILDING COMPANY
HOUSTON, TEXAS
DE-103   22-NOVEMBER-1942

U.S.S. STEWART (DE 238)
VESSEL LEAVING WAYS
BROWN SHIPBUILDING COMPANY
HOUSTON, TEXAS
22-8   22 - NOVEMBER - 1942

USS *Stewart* was launched down the ways into the water in Houston on November 22, 1942. (USNHHC.)

U.S.S. STEWART(DE238)

May 31, 1943

DAY'S ORDERS

0915   Crew mustered by division Chief Petty Officers. All Hands to be
        present.
                Uniform: men - Undress whites with neckerchiefs.
                        CPO - Service Dress Whites (if available) or Khaki.
        When muster has been taken - march to the ship under charge of
        DE COTTES, CBM.
0930   Divisions take station on the fantail as directed by the Executive
        Officer. The watch detail will be stationed forward of the crew
        by the Chief Boatswain's Mate. It will be augmented by two side
        boys detailed from the First Division. The Gangway Watch, Dock
        Sentry, and Gangway Messenger will have provided themselves with
        belts for sidearms. The Dock Sentry will wear leggins. The
        Engineering Watch will carry dungarees and place them below. The
        Communications Officer will provide equipment for the Gangway Watch.
        He will also station and provide details at the Jack, Colors, and
        Commission pennant. The Gunnery Officer will provide sidearms for
        the Gangway Watch and Dock Sentry.
                The crew will be formed facing inboard and aft; Division
        Officers in front of their respective divisions.
1000   (About) 1. Commissioning Officer comes on board.
                2. Bugler sounds attention.
                3. When the Commissioning Party is ready, the Executive
                    Officer orders "Attention to Orders".
                4. The Commissioning Officer places the ship in commission.
                5. The Executive Officer orders "Right and left, face".
                    (Division Officers preface the command of execution with
                    the appropriate order).
                6. Bugler sounds "attention", "colors" and "carry on". Run
                    up colors, jack and commission pennant on first note of
                    "colors" (jack not to be two-blocked ahead of the
                    ensign).
                7. The Executive Officer orders "Divisions, right and left
                    face".
                8. The Prospective Commanding Officer reads his orders
                    and letter from the Secretary of the Navy.
                9. Remarks by the Commanding Officer and the Commissioning
                    Officer.
                10. Commanding Officer orders "Set the Watch". Executive
                    Officer orders Boatswain's Mate to post the watch. The
                    Chief Boatswain's Mate advances a few feet, pipes, and
                    passes the word, "Now go to your stations all the
                    regular port details, first section.". Watch takes
                    stations.
                11. Honors rendered as the Commissioning Officer leaves the
                    ship.
                12. Divisions will be dismissed by "retreat" on the bugle.

When directed: - Division fall in on shore and march to the Receiving Station.
        Change clothes and finish being paid. Watch reliefs eat
        early. Duty Chief Petty Officer obtain written request
        from Executive Officer.

USS *Stewart's* day's orders for commissioning day, May 31 1943, left nothing to chance. The
skipper put out distinct directions as to how the crew of *Stewart*, the newest destroyer escort,
would receive the commissioning party on her special day. (AUWC.)

Stewart's officers came aboard and were ready to take command of the ship, which, for the first few months, took them up and down the East Coast and to Bermuda, back to Philadelphia, down to Miami, and then to Norfolk, Virginia. (GO.)

UNITED STATES NAVAL RESERVE

Midshipmen's School

NEW YORK, N.Y.

THIS IS TO CERTIFY THAT

MIDSHIPMAN *Earl George Obern*

HAS SUCCESSFULLY COMPLETED THE COURSE AT THE UNITED STATES NAVAL RESERVE MIDSHIPMEN'S SCHOOL, NEW YORK AND HAS BEEN COMMISSIONED AS AN ENSIGN *D-70 (G)* UNITED STATES NAVAL RESERVE.

Dec. 2, 1942.
(Date)

Captain, United States Navy
Commanding Officer

Officer training had many facets, as it does today, from officer accession training, to technical training, to training aboard ship at sea. This Midshipmen's School certificate for Ens. Earl George Obern, dated December 2, 1942, shows how new to their jobs many of the young officers were as ships set out to meet the enemy. (GO.)

ANCHOR WINDLASS

GREASING OF ANCHOR WINDLASS IS
CARRIED OUT BY AN ANCHOR DETAIL AS
SET DOWN IN SHIP'S ORGANIZATION.
AUXILLIARY GANG MAKES WEEKLY
INSPECTION TO ASCERTAIN WHETHER
OR NOT MACHINERY IS BEING GREASED
EFFICIENTLY AND SUFFICIENTLY ——
ELECTRICAL DEP'T. HAS GREASING AND
OILING OF ELECTRIC MOTORS AND GEAR

INSPECTED FOR LUBRICATION - OK

INSPECTED FOR LUBRICATION - OK.

INSPECTED FOR LUBRICATION - OK

INSPECTED FOR LUBRICATION - OK

INSPECTED FOR LUBRICATION - OK

INSPECTED FOR LUBRICATION - OK

INSPECTED FOR LUBRICATION - OK

USS *Stewart* raised anchor with Lt. Comdr. B.C. Turner in command on June 10, 1943, headed for Galveston, where ironically she would return about 30 years later. A few days later, *Stewart* reported in to join the 8th Naval District in New Orleans to conduct shake down training. (AUWC.)

Prior to shoving off, key systems like the engine room power controls in the aft engine room of USS *Stewart* needed to be tested, with the necessary supplies and tools on hand. (AUWC.)

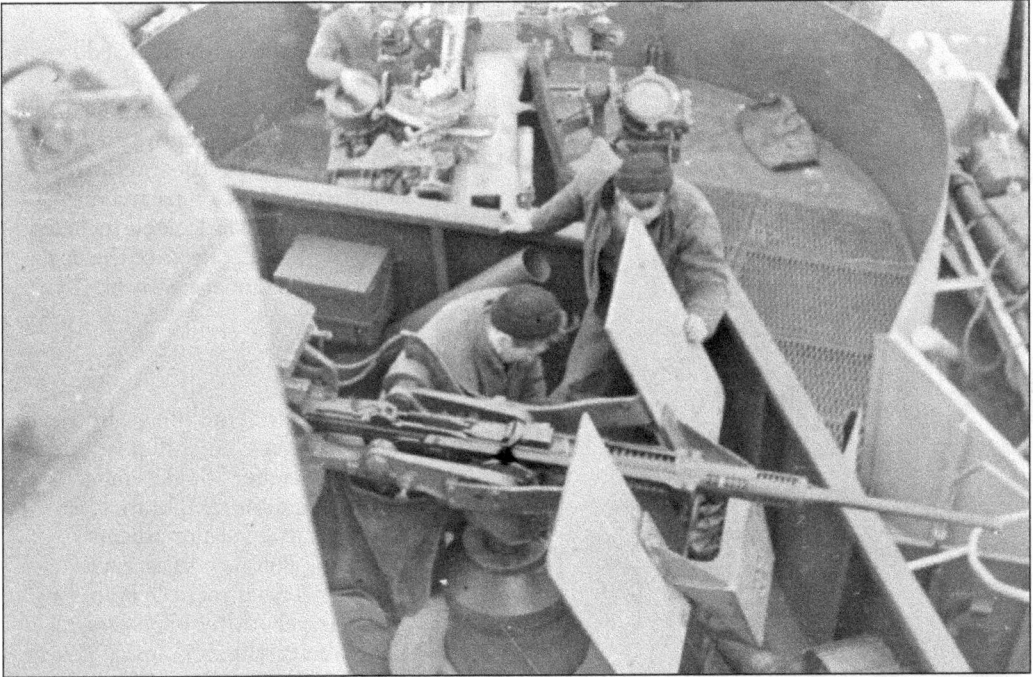

Destroyer escort crews had to ensure the 3-inch guns, as well as the 40mm and 20mm anti-aircraft guns, were cleaned and well maintained. Their lives depended on it. On the right-hand side of the picture, note the "cage" that held the life raft. These cages were positioned throughout the ship. (RB.)

Bunk assignments are critical to a sailor's personal success. Three bunks to a berthing rack were common for ranks up to some of the more senior enlisted petty officers. (KC.)

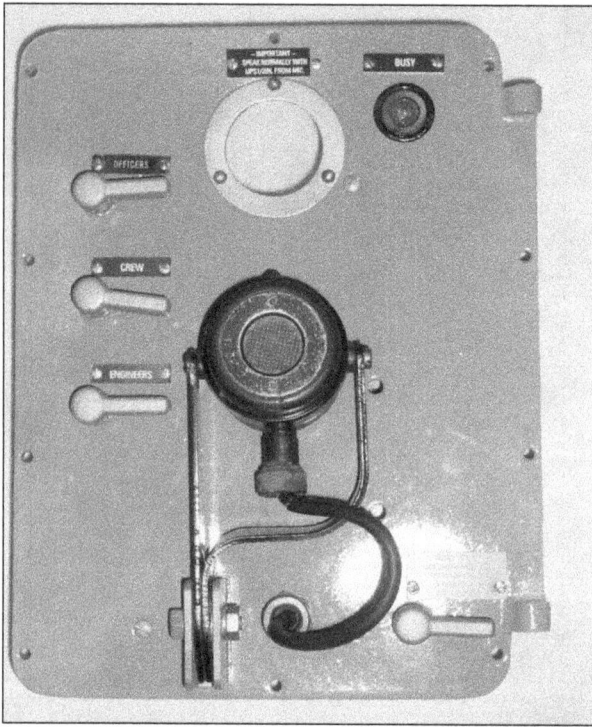

USS *Stewart's* 1MC (1 Main Circuit) is the main public address system for the ship. It is used to transmit daily orders and general information to the entire crew, from the decks to the interior compartments. Compartments where a 1MC was located included the pilot house, officer of the day station, and damage control. (KC.)

Joseph Stalin, Franklin D. Roosevelt, and Winston Churchill pose during their November 28–December 1, 1943, summit in Tehran. USS *Stewart* carried senior officers down the Potomac in escort of the presidential yacht of Franklin D. Roosevelt. After relocating all personnel to the USS *Iowa*, *Stewart* continued escort duties across much of the Atlantic. (LOC.)

Destroyer escorts routinely enduring varied routes through rough sailing during their voyages around the Atlantic or Caribbean. On May 3, 1944, *Stewart* sailed with a convoy from Aruba around South America to the Panama Canal Zone. From there, she escorted another convoy to Guantanamo Bay, Cuba, and on to Bermuda alone for experimental testing and training. (USNHHC.)

This aerial view of USS *Stewart* at sea off the coast of North Carolina on November 21, 1943, provides a clear view of her armament. Aft of the anchors are two 3-inch, 50-caliber guns. Behind the most forward gun is the Hedgehog depth charge system. There are multiple stations of 20mm and 40mm anti-aircraft guns, and aft is a third 3-inch gun. (USNHHC.)

14 May 1944.

SURFACE SHIP SCHEDULE - SUNDAY (4th DAY).

RUN NO.	DEPTH	ATTACK SHIP	WEAPON	TYPE
1	90-330	STEWART	H/H	Single
2	"	"	"	"
3	"	"	"	"
4	"	"	DC	"
5	"	"	"	"
6	"	"	"	"
7	"	WAINWRIGHT	DC	"
8	"	"	"	"
9	"	"	"	"
10	"	"	"	"
11	"	"	"	Coordinated
12	"	STEWART	"	"
13	"	WAINWRIGHT	"	"
14	"	STEWART	H/H	"
15	"	WAINWRIGHT	DC	"
16	"	STEWART	H/H	"
17	"	WAINWRIGHT	DC	"
18	"	STEWART	DC	"
19	"	WAINWRIGHT	DC	"

C. E. WEAKLEY.

Here, USS *Stewart* is off the coast of New York on February 25, 1945. To the port and starboard sides are eight MK-6 (K-gun) depth charge launchers and two racks at the stern to roll depth charges off the back. One difference between these photographs is that in 1943, *Stewart* had three 21-inch torpedo launchers amidships. They were replaced with more 40mm guns in 1945. (USNHHC.)

USS *Stewart* and the Sims-class destroyer USS *Wainwright* (DD-419) conducted experimental attacks on the captured Italian submarine *Rea*. Here is the surface ship schedule for Sunday, May 14, 1944. During that time, *Stewart* participated in a search off Bermuda for an unidentified radio direction finder contact and made a depth charge attack with inconclusive results. (AUWC.)

The young men who made up destroyer escort crews needed to be versatile and courageous. On April 10, 1945, USS *Stewart* and USS *Edsall* escorted a convoy returning from Liverpool, England. The SS *Nashbulk* accidentally rammed the tanker SS *St. Mihiel*, full of aviation fuel. The DEs put out the fires, rescued survivors, and reestablished operations of a ship four times its size. (RS.)

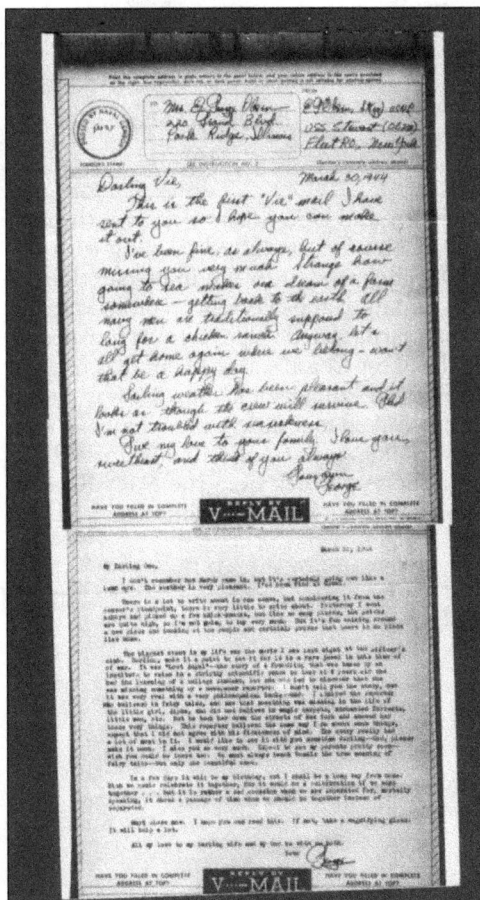

World War II sailors sent Victory Mail, or "V-Mail" back home. V-Mail letters were censored, photographed onto microfilm, and then reprinted on paper at their destination for delivery. Here, an ensign on the *Stewart* tells his wife he thinks about having a farm, and tells her, "there is a lot to write about in one sense, but considering it from the censor's standpoint, there is very little to write about." (GO.)

After saving SS *St. Mihiel*, *Stewart* accompanied USS *Edsall* and USS *Moore* (DE-240) through the Panama Canal to Pearl Harbor in early August 1945. *Stewart* conducted training with the submarine USS *Spearfish* (SS-190) and heavy cruiser USS *Baltimore* (CA-68) in preparation for the land invasion of Japan. *Stewart's* role was rumored to be part of a "picket fence;" protecting the landing forces from attacks by air and by submarine. Japan surrendered before *Stewart* finished its training. On September 5, 1945, *Stewart* departed for the West Coast and the Canal Zone, and finally, she reported for duty to the Atlantic Reserve Fleet in Philadelphia. *Stewart* was placed out of commission and sat in the reserve fleet for over 20 years in four different locations: Green Cove Springs, Florida; Charleston, South Carolina; Norfolk, Virginia; and finally, in 1969, in Orange, Texas, close to where she was originally built. She was struck from the Navy Register in 1972 and donated to Seawolf Park as part of its World War II Naval Museum memorial two years later. (ML.)

Five

RESTORING THE WARSHIPS

In the early 1970s, the US Navy donated the USS *Cavalla* submarine and USS *Stewart* destroyer escort to the City of Galveston as museum artifacts in good working order. Over the next 25 years, through inadequate preservation, the city allowed the vessels to deteriorate. In October 1998, meetings were held to decide whether to replace the ships with an RV park.

Word went out to submarine veterans across the nation, and in one voice, they said, "Save the *Cavalla*!" Veterans wrote essays and articles, set up donation websites, and organized rallies. The rallies caught the eye of local "salty dogs" and philanthropists like George Strake Jr.; songwriter Jeff Morris even penned a song, "Saga of the *Cavalla*." Led by famed naval game developer Neal Stevens, former *Cavalla* captain Ernest "Zeke" Zelmer, nuclear sub captain Zeb Alford, and other veterans and volunteers, enough money was raised to restore *Cavalla* to museum standards.

Also in 1998, the nonprofit Cavalla Historical Foundation (CHF) formed to oversee the restoration of the *Cavalla* and *Stewart* with MCPO John McMichael hired as full-time curator.

Twenty years later, a new crew of volunteers and staff has taken up the gauntlet of restoration, preservation, and education at the naval museum at Seawolf Park. Organizations such as the Edsall Class Veterans Association (ECVA), US Submarine Veterans (USSVI), Texas A&M Galveston Maritime Academy, and the Brazos Valley Amateur Radio Club all spend time and sweat making the warships of Seawolf Park safe and presentable to the visiting public. Both the ECVA and the Lone Star WW2 Living History Crew (World War II re-enactors) call the museum their home.

In 2017 alone, volunteers like college students Victoria Crooks and Asher Spaulding, veterans CPO Mac Christy and SSgt Bryan Fitch, and groups from the Boy Scouts to the Rotary have given over 5,000 hours of their time to repair, clean, scrape, and paint these two historic ships.

For two decades after USS *Cavalla* and USS *Stewart* were donated by the US Navy to the US Submarine Veterans of World War II and the City of Galveston, little was done to preserve the ships. The next set of pictures clearly show how neglect, storm surge, and weathering caused severe damage both inside and out. (AUWC.)

Gaping holes made USS *Cavalla*'s infrastructure suspect for safe visiting. Her deck was infused with concrete, which caused oxidation and deterioration. Volunteers had to tear out *Cavalla*'s deck area aft of the bridge and rebuild the submarine superstructure. Much of the piping and structures found between the pressure hull and the deck had to be restored or replaced. Thankfully, the bridge and sail maintained structural integrity. (AUWC.)

USS *Stewart* sustained damage after constant weathering with little preventive maintenance. Hurricanes like Ike and Harvey surged against both ships, soaking each to the lower interior levels. "Rust never sleeps," and it has not let up for over 45 years. (AUWC.)

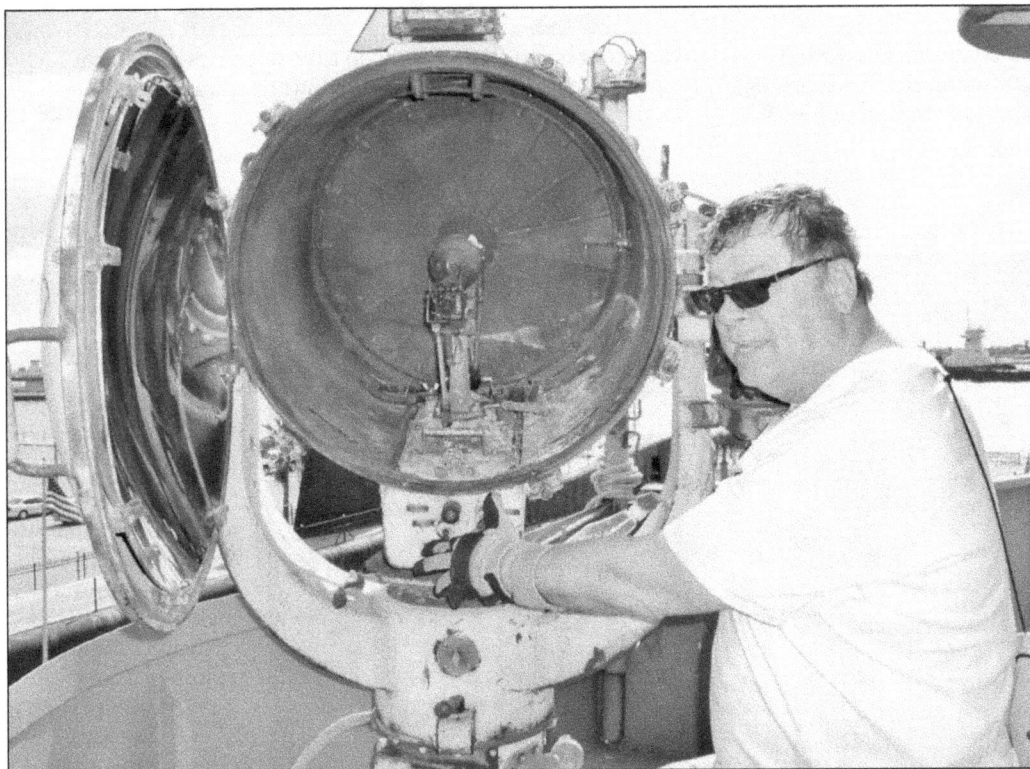

USS *Stewart* volunteer Pete Lohmer is working on the signal lantern. Water damage after major storms occurred when neglect allowed pin-sized rust holes to develop. Water and salty air start to eat away at all things metal at sea and when surrounded by sea water. (AUWC.)

USS *Cavalla's* bow nose caved in due to stress on former torpedo tube openings and storm surge. US submarine veterans again promised to intervene in the downward spiral of the *Cavalla's* physical condition. (AUWC.)

Berthing on USS *Stewart* lacked mattresses (water seepage caused mold and mildew), and mess tables were destroyed. Sailors enjoined a new support group, the ECVA, to focus on restoring and preserving the DE to its World War II splendor. (AUWC.)

Another challenge to the continued preservation of the warships of Seawolf Park was vandalism. Prior to the reconstruction period, visitors seeking souvenirs from World War II would pry off almost anything they could. Of particular desire was anything from the forward or aft torpedo rooms. A cage had to be installed to keep artifacts inside the submarine. (AUWC.)

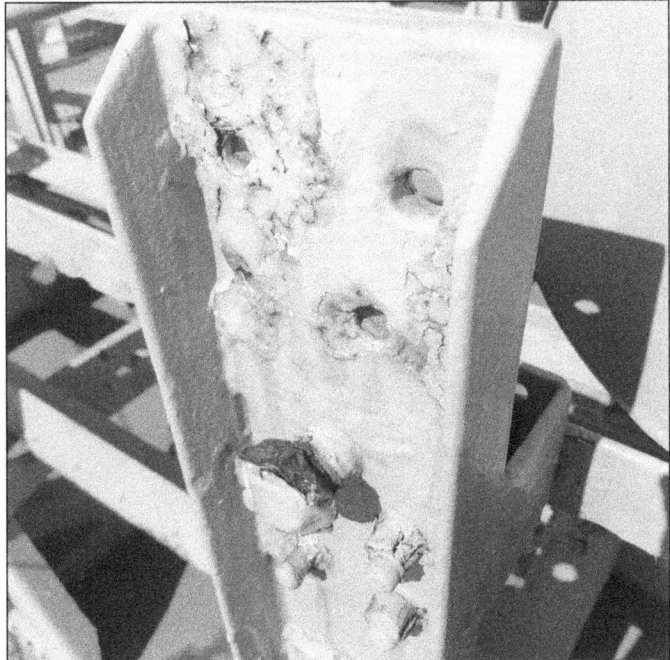

Due to the neglected state of the ships, the US Navy was deciding whether to pull them back under Navy control. Concerned submarine veterans and historians claimed that the park board never allotted enough funds toward preserving *Cavalla*. They charged that the area submarine veterans' group was not actively participating in restoration efforts, and revenues generated by the naval display dropped steadily. Something had to be done. (KC.)

Names that should make their way into the Cavalla Historical Foundation Hall of Fame include Neal Stevens, Dave Stoops, Gil Raynor, and retired Navy captains Zeke Zellmer and Zeb Alford. They all put their sweat and time into fundraising, organizational structure, and physical restoration efforts. (AUWC.)

USS Cavalla received a new wooden deck, her hull was restored, and she was given a nice set of ribbons signifying her achievements in war. Work weekends would be called, and people would show. (AUWC.)

Cavalla reunions held annually helped raise awareness and donations. The Galveston Park Board reversed course and committed significant donations toward the replacement of Cavalla's deck. The nonprofit Cavalla Historical Foundation was formed in 1999 to oversee the naval museum's operations, and a new executive director was hired to run operations. (AUWC.)

Restoration of the two ships at Seawolf Park shifted to a new generation of submariners and Edsall-class DE sailors. Many of the senior volunteers of the 1990s and 2000s were no longer capable of safely climbing ladders or using power tools. (AUWC.)

For a while, naval museum operations held steady, like a well-maintained diesel engine on a brand-new destroyer escort. But it would not last, as the submariners and the surface ship veterans each had their favorite vessel. Neglect started to rear its ugly head again. (AUWC.)

USS *Stewart's* aft steering room was not showable to the public due mostly to neglect. While the majority of restoration efforts went to resurrect *Cavalla* to museum quality, *Stewart* started to succumb to the elements. (AUWC.)

USS *Cavalla*, prior to 2008, was solidly embedded in the ground. In 2008, Hurricane Ike surged through the Galveston Island area and caused significant damage to both vessels. *Cavalla* rose off its cradle and drifted over 10 feet before settling back down, this time seated a couple of feet higher as dirt and silt had washed up under her. (RS.)

Here is USS *Cavalla* sometime after Hurricane Ike struck in 2008. In the previous picture, the aft end of the submarine was partially buried, sitting low in its subterranean cradle. Here, the aft end is almost off the ground as dirt fill swept under the submarine during the storm and now supports *Cavalla* at a higher angle. (KC)

For the last four or five years, a new restoration effort continues to build in capability. The ECVA, led by CPO Mac Christy, holds "Work Week" twice each year, when they bring in 20 to 30 volunteers to conduct restoration activities. (AUWC.)

Three of the ECVA volunteers are pictured ready to take on a new project on the USS *Stewart*. Depending on which volunteer organization each person associates with, efforts fluctuate between the sub and the ship. (AUWC.)

While the ECVA primarily focuses on the *Stewart* and the US Sub Vets group, along with some key individual volunteers, focuses on the submarine, luckily, the Texas A&M Galveston maritime cadets help fill any slack in attention. Here, the cadets are preparing to repaint the pressure hull of USS *Cavalla*. (KC.)

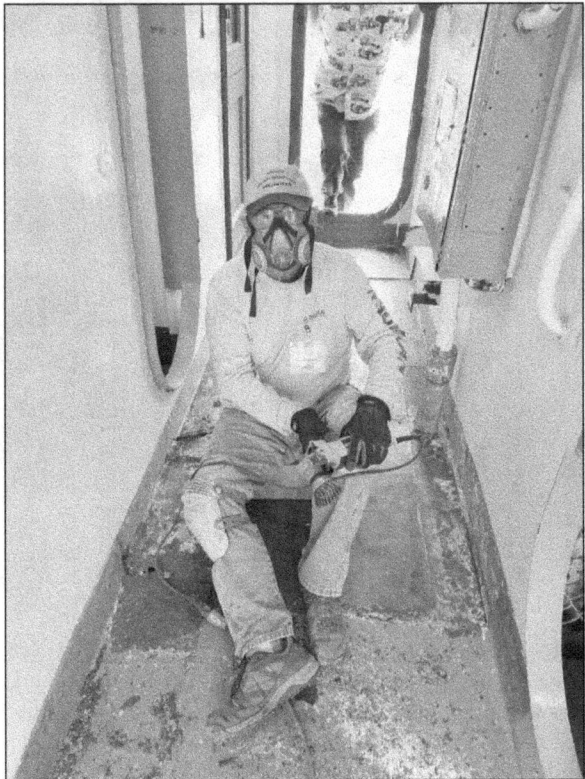

Robin Avance of the ECVA demonstrates the proper safety wear for scraping, grinding, and repainting a deck area near the B-4 engine room hatch. (KC.)

Spencer Ernst (left) and other volunteers are nearing the completion of replacing the barrels of the 40mm port gun on USS *Stewart*. When volunteers arrive from around the country for one week every six months, some projects can take over a year to complete. (KC.)

Dick Klinker of the Brazos Valley Amateur Radio Club works on *Stewart's* World War II radio sets while integrating modern ham radio transmissions from the radio room. Note the typewriter at lower right. Unlike those in civilian offices, this typewriter only used capital letters for faster and more efficient messaging. (KC.)

Texas A&M cadet Asher Spaulding volunteers to overhaul one of USS *Stewart's* four diesel engines as well as a 1943 air compressor. The expectation is to prepare working models of both for public display (KC.)

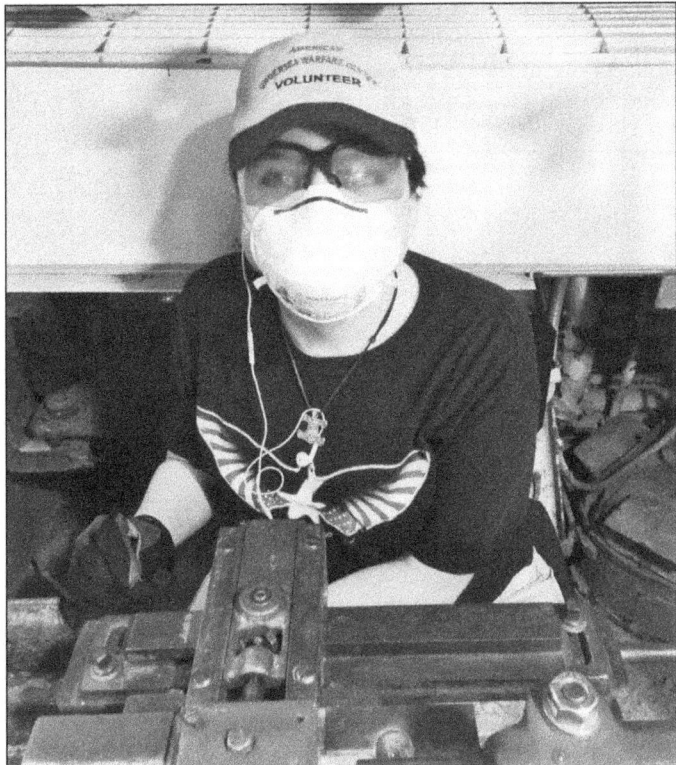

Tori Crooks dons a protective mask and goggles as she sands, grinds, polishes, and paints a lathe on USS *Cavalla*. All volunteers are expected to wear the proper protective gear when working at the naval museum. (DRKC.)

During the initial restoration efforts, the USS *Cavalla* reunion group held a ceremony honoring the officers and crew of the submarine, as well as recognizing many Galveston-area veterans and military dignitaries. This event also helped collect needed funds to finish the hull restoration efforts of *Cavalla*. Notice the earlier version of the *Cavalla's* ribbons are spaced apart; today, they are closer together. (AUWC.)

The restoration efforts of so many have made the difference between preserving an important piece of history and leveling the ground to make way for recreational vehicle parking. This picture of two 40mm gun barrels is an example of what kind of workmanship is being performed at Seawolf Park. From rusted shards of metal, they tell a story of heroism at sea. (KC.)

Six

SEAWOLF PARK TODAY

Both the USS *Cavalla* and USS *Stewart* were built quickly, expected to do battle and then be scrapped. Instead, both warships continue their battle three-quarters of a century later at the American Undersea Warfare Center at Seawolf Park. Many parts of the ships are open to the public; some of the lower decks are not due to safety concerns unless accompanied by a tour guide or staff member.

This chapter presents a photographic tour of Seawolf Park, *Cavalla*, *Stewart*, and other important artifacts and areas not normally accessible to the public.

The pictures tell a story similar to a park tour. It starts on the grounds around the ships, the Compass Rose Memorial Plaza commemorating the submarines lost at sea during World War II, the sail of the USS *Tautog* and the control tower of USS *Carp*. It then moves on deck and through the *Cavalla* from inside the sail/bridge, down to the forward torpedo room, through each compartment, and finally exiting through the aft torpedo room. With slight detours up into the control tower or down under the maneuvering room, the sense of claustrophobia is not uncommon. Knowing that over 60 submariners spent months at a time inside is eye opening.

After the *Cavalla*, pictures of the *Stewart* will seem more airy. Starting at her boarding ladder sitting between two 3-inch guns from the USS *Texas* and the *Stewart's* own propellers, visitors climb onto the quarter deck and walk aft to the stern of the ship's main deck where the tour route starts. It goes past the depth charges and 3-inch guns, through interior compartments, and to the bow of the ship to see the 2,000-pound anchors and Hedgehog depth charges. From there, the pictures show many of the interior office spaces, cabins, galley, and ward rooms where 210 sailors spent their days and nights for weeks at a time.

This chapter starts with diagrams of a Gato-class submarine and Edsall-class destroyer escort.

Pictured is a cutaway of a World War II attack submarine. The virtual tour of USS *Cavalla* takes one down the bow hatch to the forward torpedo room and through the upper deck of the submarine. Below deck are the battery compartments, the lower part of the diesel engines, storage, and the propulsion motors. (AUWC.)

The USS *Cavalla* lies in dry berthing facing the Galveston Channel. She is on the port side of the USS *Stewart*. (KC.)

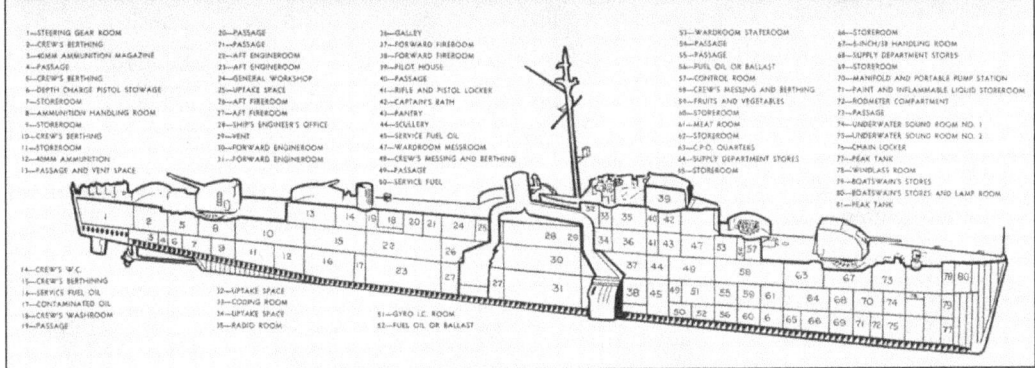

This is a cutaway of a World War II destroyer escort. The virtual tour of USS *Stewart* takes one to the aft fantail, through the interior compartments of the main deck, to the bow of the ship. It will then explore the lower decks, followed by the upper decks. (AUWC.)

USS *Stewart* sits in a dry berth also facing east toward the channel and the US Coast Guard Station across the water. (KC.)

Central to Seawolf Park and the Naval Museum, located between the historic World War II submarine and destroyer escort, is Memorial Plaza. Walking the grounds, visitors see memorials to USS *Seawolf*, Captain Kopp and his Army special forces lost with *Seawolf*, and each of the other 51 submarine crews lost at sea. In the center of the plaza is a compass rose, encircled by plaques

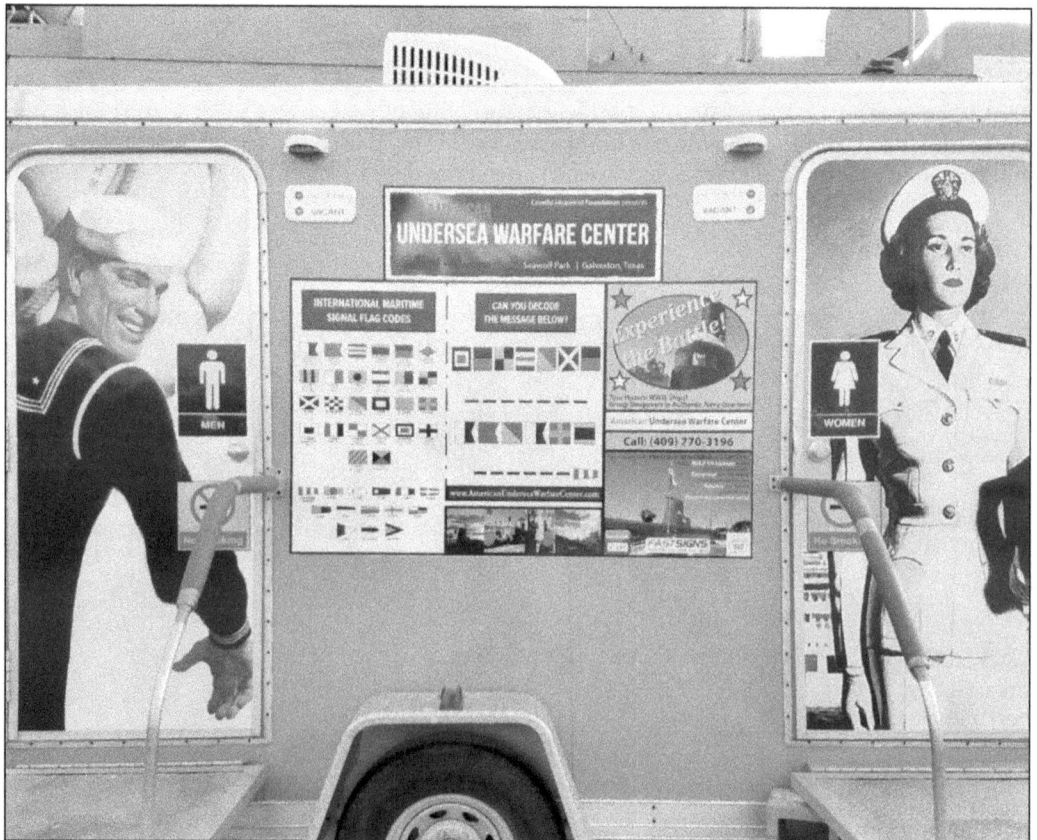

Information abounds around Memorial Plaza and the grounds of the naval museum. From memorial plaques, to information boards on the specifics of each ship, to even the air conditioned restroom trailer, visitors learn at every turn. (KC.)

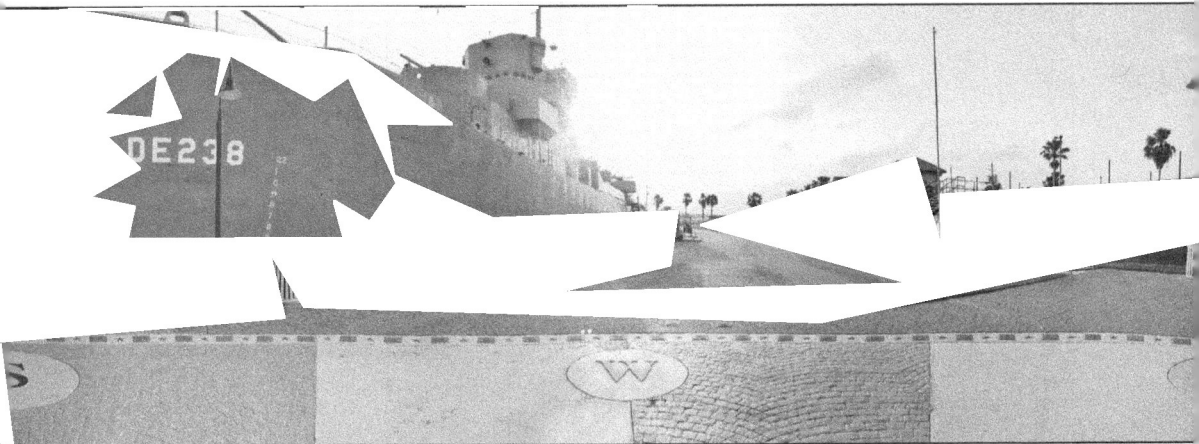

honoring each of the submarines that include the date and location where that submarine was sent on eternal patrol. On display in front of *Cavalla* is a Mark XVI torpedo used during World War II. All around the naval museum, visitors can watch local anglers work their fishing magic trying to snag a passing flounder or red fish. (KC.)

Each hour, Seawolf Park is viewed by hundreds of visitors passing by between Galveston and Port Bolivar aboard the car ferry connecting these two beach areas. (KC.)

Looking forward past the entrance hatch and the emergency exit hatch and over the bow of *Cavalla*, the conning tower of USS *Carp* (left) and the Galveston Channel are in view. Across the channel are the US Coast Guard station, the University of Texas Medical Branch, and twin condominium towers on East Beach. The *Carp's* hatch may be opened to see where periscopes are positioned. (KC.)

Cavalla Foundation officers Capt. Gary Bell (right) and Comdr. Bryan Lethcoe provide a visitor to Seawolf Park a special tour inside the USS *Carp* conning tower. *Carp* was a World War II Balao-class submarine that was awarded a battle star for her service. (KC.)

The deck of the *Cavalla* is wood suspended over a large hollow tube. World War II submarines were double-hull boats. Inside the main pressure hull were the compartments that contained most of the equipment and living spaces. Wrapped around that inner hull were a series of tanks that formed the outer hull. This supported the superstructure, the bridge and sail, and the guns. (KC.)

Take a peek below the teak. Below the wooden planks are the fuel and lube oil tanks, trim tanks, and ballast tanks. (KC.)

The hatch leading to the forward torpedo room was not meant for submariners, but to load torpedoes into the sub on greased skids. In World War II, they would load 16 torpedoes forward, with six of those into the tubes. (USNHHC.)

The forward torpedo room was renovated after World War II as the Navy experimented with newer sonar and hydrophonic technology and equipment. Two of the tubes were removed for experimental equipment. The firing tubes are made of brass and bronze. Pictured here are a series of levers and vents to control the compressed air used when firing the torpedoes. (KC.)

In this view, looking up into the forward torpedo room, is one of the main entrances to the submarine as well as one of the main escape hatches. It can hold up to half a dozen sailors who would climb in, close the hatch inside, and open the outer hatch to escape. After the previous group escaped, those waiting would use levers to open and close the hatch to drain the water. (KC.)

The pitometer is connected to a propeller on the boat. It records the speed and distance traveled; over 36,000 nautical miles since *Cavalla's* last commissioning. The sound head shaft suspends and rotates the sound head, which is the "ping" heard as the sub searches for targets. (KC.)

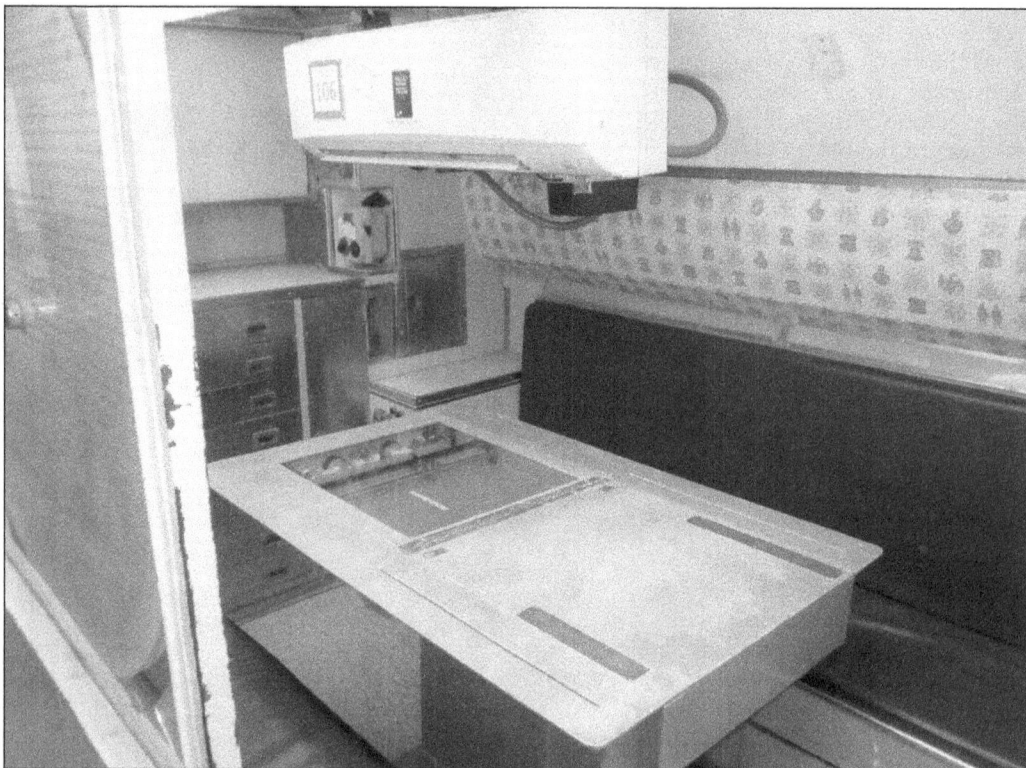

"Officer's country" includes the pantry, wardroom, captain's and officer's quarters, and the admin office. The pantry received food from the galley and served six to eight officers. When supplies came on board, they were stashed everywhere: potatoes were put in shower stalls, coffee went behind the diesels, and canned fruits were behind every pipe. The crew literally had to eat their way to the deck. (KC.)

The last room in this compartment is the yeoman's office, where the sub's administrative work was done. It was quite small and required a lot of organizational skills. Here is where personal supplies like candy, gum, and toiletries could be purchased. (KC.)

The control room was the operations center of the *Cavalla* and included the controls for the high- and low-pressure air systems used to blow ballast tanks, the systems that dive the boat, the radio room, and an emergency steering station. In the middle is the gyroscopic compass. The sub's steel structure affected normal magnetic compasses, but gyrocompasses used an electrically powered, fast-spinning gyroscope wheel to identify true north. (AUWC.)

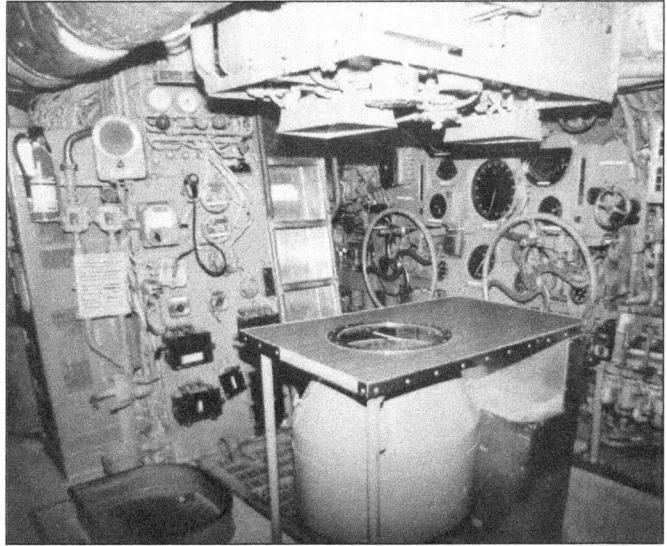

The conning tower housed two periscopes used for locating and targeting. It linked to the telegraph, compass, collision alarm, pitometer, radar, and sonar controls. It was connected to the torpedo rooms through the targeting data computer (TDC). The TDC calculates the firing solution (speed, range, and bearing) of the torpedoes and feeds that data to the torpedo to be fired. This is also the main steering room. (KC.)

Guests sitting in the mess watching a movie on USS *Cavalla* include Sam Herman Kossler, left, grandson of the first captain of the sub, Herman Kossler. The aft battery houses the galley, the crew's mess, and the crew's quarters. Below this deck are spaces for refrigerated and nonperishable food storage, the munitions locker, and another bank of batteries. The galley served three meals a day plus 24-hour snacks and coffee. (KC.)

The main crew quarters were where most of the enlisted men slept. They kept all their personal gear in small lockers lining the bulkhead. Because the sub was in 24-hour operations, there were always crew members in sleep mode. This room was kept at minimum light levels and quiet, so many of the crew would read or write letters home. (KC.)

The forward engine room housed two water distillers that turned 750 gallons of salt water into fresh water daily. Fresh water was used to recharge the batteries and for cooking and hygiene. The aft engine room included oil purifiers and centrifuges to separate lubricants from sea water used to keep the oil tanks filled. Four 1,600-horsepower diesel engines filled out the rest of the space. (KC.)

The maneuvering room housed the equipment to control electric power for propulsion from either the batteries or diesels. The main power cubicle acted like power transformers. Further aft is the power control station, where two electrician's mates operated the port and starboard side motors using multiple control levers. The main propulsion motors that drove the propellers were located below in the motor room. (KC.)

The aft torpedo room was the last compartment in the boat. Like the forward torpedo room, it had Mark XIV torpedoes brought in on skids, with four loaded into the tubes. Another four torpedoes were stored on racks. Aft torpedoes were considered primarily defensive in nature. They were a means to attack another ship or sub in pursuit. (KC.)

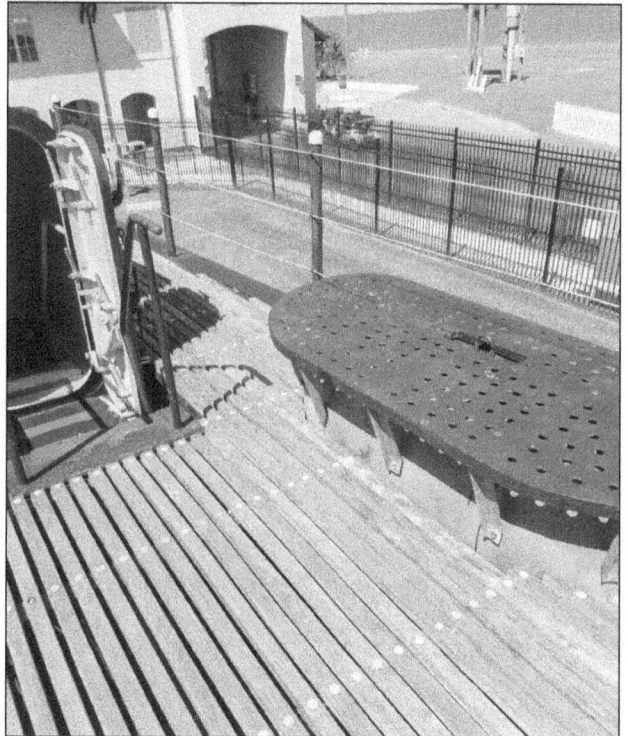

Returning topside of USS Cavalla, a bench sits on the port side of the deck. This was an emergency buoy to be launched to help locate and rescue the submarine in case of damage or malfunction. (KC.)

USS *Stewart* is 307 feet long and 37 feet across, and its draft is 12 feet. Displacing about 1,500 tons, she housed a crew of 201 sailors and 8 officers. *Stewart's* two bronze 56-inch propellers each weigh over a ton and were powered by two diesel engines to drive the ship to 21 knots. Behind the propellers are two 3-inch, 50-caliber memorial guns donated from the USS *Texas*. (KC.)

The quarterdeck was the designated area next to the boarding ladder where one would request permission to come aboard from the officer of the day. It was customary when boarding any ship where the flag is flying to halt at the gangway, face aft, and salute the flag. Visitors then salute the officer of the day, holding the salute until it was returned with permission granted. (KC.)

The anti-submarine weapons at the after deck, or fantail, are the depth charges and MK6 depth charge projectors (or K-guns). Depth charges were rolled off the racks at the back of the ship or were fired off by the K-guns over each side of the ship. This configuration dropped 200-pound explosive charges in oval patterns at 60 or 90 yards behind the ship as it pushed forward. (KC.)

USS *Stewart* had three 3-inch, 50-caliber guns, two forward and one aft. Manned by seven-man gun crews, they fired 13-pound shells up to eight miles. Hedgehogs behind the gun were used to attack submerged submarines ahead of the ship. Twenty-four 65-pound projectiles would be launched 250 yards out in an oval pattern. They would explode on contact, rupturing the pressure hull of an enemy submarine. (KC.)

Along the interior passageway toward the bow of the ship was the crews' head, or latrine. Showers, toilets, and wash bins were separated to allow maximum use. With 200 sailors needing to use these facilities at various times, privacy and luxury were nonexistent. A shower would consist of a 30-second rinse, lather with the water off, and another 30-second rinse. It was the same with shaving. (KC.)

Along the passageway was the engineering log room, or damage control. During an emergency, this was where all the key documents and blueprints were kept. The ship's store was on the port side of this passageway. This is where sailors purchased items needed for hygiene, cigarettes, candy, and other personal items. Any profits supported morale and recreation. (KC.)

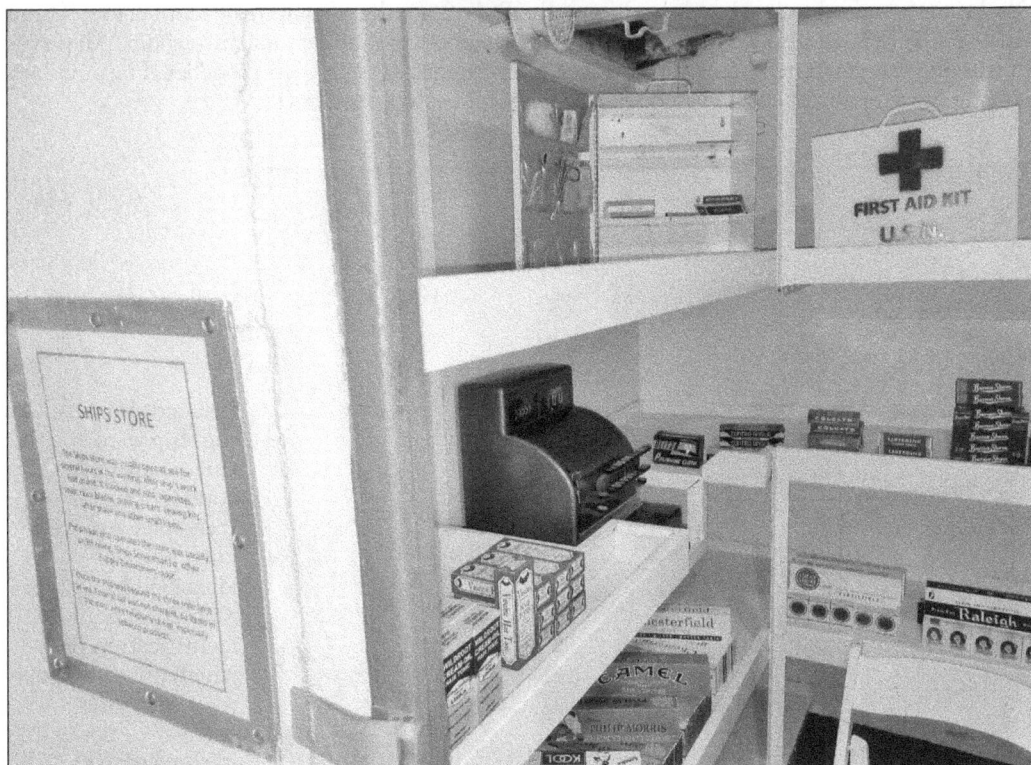

On the starboard side was a hatch leading to the B-4 aft auxiliary equipment room below. Three other similar hatches also led to either a main engine room or auxiliary machine room. All power for the ship was generated here by four large diesel engines, two for each propeller. The auxiliary equipment tied pairs of engines to one drive shaft for each propeller. (KC.)

Located throughout the ship were emergency power connections for three-phase power. Each phase is identified by 1, 2, or 3 notches to allow identification of which phase is which when plugging into emergency power in the dark. (KC.)

Ship's cooks prepared three meals daily for 210 individuals. Food was stored in the "refers," or refrigerator, and cooked in the galley. Meals were carried to mess decks one pot at a time, where it was served. Cooks made the food in ovens and these large kettles known as "coppers." Imagine pots simmering with soup or coffee, ovens filled with freshly baked bread, and aromas wafting across the decks. (KC.)

Forward of the galley were the officers' pantry, ward room, and staterooms. The ward room is where officers had meetings, relaxed, and ate. It had a small library, a safe for classified documents, and drawers to store charts and maps. During battle stations, the ward room and table had a secondary use as an operating table for the ship's surgeon. (KC.)

123

The bow of the ship included the forecastle, or "foc'sle," and the "ground tackle," or anchoring system. Unless part of the anchor crew, sailors would not have been up there when they dropped anchor, as it was easy to get caught in the chain. Anchors weighing one ton were tethered to about 660 feet of chain and raised and lowered by a hydraulic winch assembly, the windlass. (KC.)

On the O1 deck (one level above the main deck) is the ship's office, the captain's cabin located next door, and the ship's main communications center (pictured), which housed the radio transmitters and receivers. Ideally, the captain could send and receive messages quickly and have close access to the bridge or pilot house. (KC.)

On the O2 deck above the captain's cabin is the ship's pilot house. A helmsman operated the ship's wheel and took orders from the officer of the deck. Orders to the engine rooms were transmitted from here, and a binnacle with magnetic and gyro compass behind the wheel indicated the ship's direction of travel. For quick communication with the combat information center (CIC), captain's quarters, and the flying bridge above, the brass voice tubes overhead were used. (KC.)

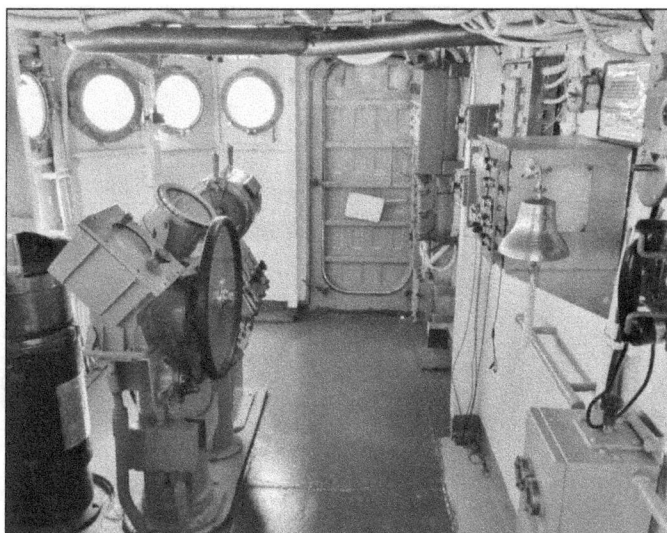

The CIC was off limits to any sailor without clearance. All of the ship's radar, sonar, and communications data was collected, interpreted, and plotted for navigation, attacking the enemy, and defending the ship in this compartment. This information was provided directly to the captain on the flying bridge. (KC.)

The O1 gun deck also had the smoke stack and the Bofors 40mm and Oerlikon 20mm anti-aircraft guns, as well as life rafts and a practice 3-inch gun loader. The 40mm guns required from four to seven crewmen to load, aim, fire, and recover spent shells. They could fire two to three rounds every second, with a maximum range of four to five miles. (KC.)

Below the main deck were the crew's mess, petty officer's quarters, the windlass room, and storage lockers. In the middle of the crew's mess was a hatch that led farther down to the gyroscope (pictured) and sonar rooms. (KC.)

126

BIBLIOGRAPHY

Beach, Edward L., Commander, US Navy. *Submarine!*. New York, NY: Henry Holt and Company, 1952.

Chant, Christopher. *Submarines of the 20th Century*. London, UK: Tiger Books, 1996.

Harris, Brayton. *The Navy Times Book of Submarines, a Political, Social, and Military History*. New York, NY: Berkley Publishing Group, 1997.

Parker, A. Leland. *Honoring Seawolf & The Submariners Lost During WWII*. Corpus Christi, TX: South Coast Publishing, 1983.

Sieber, Bill. *From Groton to Galveston, S.S. 244–U.S.S. Cavalla*. Windsor, CT: WLS, 1979.

Visit us at
arcadiapublishing.com

www.ingramcontent.com/pod-product-compliance
Lightning Source LLC
Chambersburg PA
CBHW080911100426
42812CB00007B/2237